ENVIRONMENTAL SCIENCE

DANTES/DSST* Test Study Guide

All rights reserved. This Study Guide, Book and Flashcards are protected under the US Copyright Law. No part of this book or study guide or flashcards may be reproduced, distributed or stored in a retrieval system, or transmitted in any form or by any means, electronic, mechanical, photocopying, recording, or otherwise, without the prior written permission of the publisher Breely Crush Publishing, LLC.

© 2026 Breely Crush Publishing, LLC

*DSST is a registered trademark of The Thomson Corporation and its affiliated companies, and does not endorse this book.

971010620143

Copyright ©2003 - 2026, Breely Crush Publishing, LLC.

All rights reserved.

This Study Guide, Book and Flashcards are protected under the US Copyright Law. No part of this publication may be reproduced, distributed or stored in a retrieval system, or transmitted in any form or by any means, electronic, mechanical, photocopying, recording, or otherwise, without the prior written permission of the publisher Breely Crush Publishing, LLC.

Published by Breely Crush Publishing, LLC
10808 River Front Parkway
South Jordan, UT 84095
www.breelycrushpublishing.com

ISBN-10: 1-61433-662-8
ISBN-13: 978-1-61433-662-4

Printed and bound in the United States of America.

DSST is a registered trademark of The Thomson Corporation and its affiliated companies, and does not endorse this book.

Table of Contents

Environmental Impacts *1*
   Power Creation *1*
   Human Population Growth *2*
   Global Climate and the Greenhouse Effect *2*
   Pollution *7*
   Environmental Risk Assessment *7*
   Acid Rain *7*
   Nonpoint Source Pollution *9*
   Ozone *10*
   Eutrophication *13*
   Deforestation and Desertification *14*
Ecological Concepts *14*
   Environmental Science *14*
   Ecosystems *14*
   Biomes and Terrestrial Communities *15*
   Roles of Organisms and Food Chain *16*
   Biogeochemical Cycling *16*
   Wastewater Treatment *18*
   Trophic Levels *18*
   Energy Flow *20*
   Biodiversity *20*
   Population *20*
   Birth Rate and Death Rate *21*
   Biodiversity and Sustainability *22*
   Evolution *23*
   Agricultural and Industrial Revolutions *23*
   Succession on Land and in Freshwater *24*
Environmental Management and Conservation *24*
   Renewable and Nonrenewable Resources *24*
   The Green Revolution *25*
   Pesticides and Pest Control *25*
   Soil Conservation *26*
   Land Use *27*
   Air Pollution *27*
   Drinking Water Quality and Supply *32*
   Wastewater Treatment *34*
   Municipal Solid Waste (MSW) *36*
   Recycling *42*
   Mass Transit *43*

Political Processes and the Future *43*
  Environmental Laws, Policies and Ethics *43*
  How a Bill Becomes a Law *44*
  Differing Cultural and Societal Values *44*
Statistical Analysis of Environment *44*
  J Shape Growth Curve *44*
  S Shape Growth Curve *45*
Sample Test Questions *46*
Test-Taking Strategies *83*
Test Preparation *84*
Legal Note *84*

 Environmental Impacts

POWER CREATION

The way that we create power has an adverse effect upon the environment. Typically, we have generated power from coal burning plants which create electricity but emit harmful gas to the atmosphere as well as to the community around them. Hydro-electric power is power that is created with water. This is used in Hoover Dam, where the water is allowed to spill out and turn large turbines which create power. Wave power, although new, is also a new form of hydroelectric power. The force of the waves turn turbines which send the power generated ashore via large cables. Hydroelectric power does not emit harmful gases to the atmosphere and is generally accepted as a good form of generating power. However, it does have its limitations as not everywhere is near the ocean or has a large supply of water.

Nuclear power is a very efficient form of power creation. Nuclear power does not emit the same dangerous types of gases that are associated with coal burning power plants. However, they do produce some nuclear waste which must be controlled and stored. One of the biggest adversaries of nuclear power is public opinion and the fear of a nuclear reactor.

In the Soviet Union in 1986, the Chernobyl nuclear reactor had an explosion and melted down. The disaster resulted in harmful radioactive chemicals being released into the atmosphere over a large geographical area. The fallout from the fire and explosion was four hundred times more harmful than the Hiroshima bombing. Over 600,000 people were exposed to harmful radiation with at least 56 people died from direct exposure. After the accident, nuclear power became much less popular as the fear for individual's health and lives increased.

Coal powered electrical plants are very common to create power. Some use an electrostatic precipitator, sometimes called an electrostatic air cleaner, which filters particles from the air by creating an electric charge. They are considered very efficient because they infuse electricity only into the particles that need to be filtered and therefore use energy more effectively than other types of filters.

The United States consumes more energy per person than any other country in the world. Bangladesh uses the least amount of energy per person. Generally, the poorer and less developed a country is, the less energy is used per person.

HUMAN POPULATION GROWTH

Human population growth is a worry for many environmentalists who are concerned with today's "throw away" mentality. The earth has a carrying capacity which has not yet been defined and many people are concerned with preserving space and natural resources for future generations. As of the printing of this book, the world population was 6.89 billion people.

In the 20th century, the world saw its greatest population increase yet, and the population has continued growing. This becomes a concern as people consider that natural resources are not in infinite supply. Natural resources develop over hundreds, sometimes thousands or millions, of years. The demand is greater than the supply. Because of this, there has been a push for sustainable practices. This term means living in a way that can be continued indefinitely. This includes anything from alternate fuel sources which won't run out to growing food in personal gardens.

In 1979, China instituted a policy called the One Birth Policy. This stipulated that each family was allowed to have only one child, the purpose being to slow the population growth. The policy is reviewed every five years to determine if it will be extended another five years or not. The most recent review was in 2010 when it was decided that the policy would continue another five years. While the policy effectively slows population growth, it does create some problems. Because families can only have one child, they want sons so they can carry on the family name. This encourages discrimination, neglect, abortion, and even infanticide. It also causes an unbalanced male to female ratio within the country.

GLOBAL CLIMATE AND THE GREENHOUSE EFFECT

AN INTRODUCTION

According to the National Academy of Sciences, the Earth's surface temperature has risen by about 1 degree Fahrenheit in the past century, with accelerated warming during the past two decades. There is new and stronger evidence that most of the warming over the last 50 years is attributable to human activities. Human activities have altered the chemical composition of the atmosphere through the buildup of greenhouse gases – primarily carbon dioxide, methane, and nitrous oxide. The heat-trapping property of these gases is undisputed although uncertainties exist about exactly how earth's climate responds to them.

OUR CHANGING ATMOSPHERE

Energy from the sun drives the earth's weather and climate, and heats the earth's surface; in turn, the earth radiates energy back into space. Atmospheric greenhouse gases (water vapor, carbon dioxide, and other gases) trap some of the outgoing energy, retaining heat somewhat like the glass panels of a greenhouse.

Without this natural "greenhouse effect", temperatures would be much lower than they are now, and life as known today would not be possible. Instead, thanks to greenhouse gases, the earth's average temperature is a more hospitable 60°F. However, problems may arise when the atmospheric concentration of greenhouse gases increases.

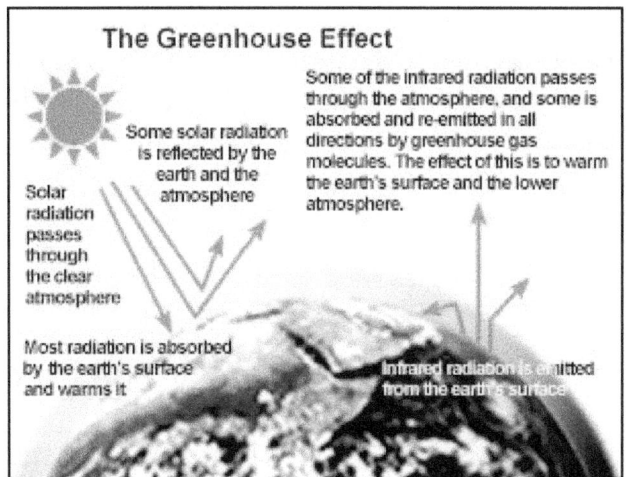

Since the beginning of the industrial revolution, atmospheric concentrations of carbon dioxide have increased nearly 30%, methane concentrations have more than doubled, and nitrous oxide concentrations have risen by about 15%. These increases have enhanced the heat-trapping capability of the earth's atmosphere. Sulfate aerosols, a common air pollutant, cool the atmosphere by reflecting light back into space; however, sulfates are short-lived in the atmosphere and vary regionally.

Why are greenhouse gas concentrations increasing? Scientists generally believe that the combustion of fossil fuels and other human activities are the primary reason for the increased concentration of carbon dioxide. Plant respiration and the decomposition of organic matter release more than 10 times the CO_2 released by human activities; but these releases have generally been in balance during the centuries leading up to the industrial revolution with carbon dioxide absorbed by terrestrial vegetation and the oceans.

What has changed in the last few hundred years is the additional release of carbon dioxide by human activities. Fossil fuels burned to run cars and trucks, heat homes and businesses, and power factories are responsible for about 98% of U.S. carbon dioxide emissions, 24% of methane emissions, and 18% of nitrous oxide emissions. Increased agriculture, deforestation, landfills, industrial production, and mining also contribute a significant share of emissions. In 1997, the United States emitted about one-fifth of total global greenhouse gases.

Estimating future emissions is difficult, because that calculation depends on demographic, economic, technological, policy, and institutional developments. Several emissions scenarios have been developed based on differing projections of these underlying factors. For example, by 2100, in the absence of emissions control policies, carbon dioxide concentrations are projected to be 30-150% higher than today's levels.

CHANGING CLIMATE

Global mean surface temperatures have increased 0.5-1.0°F since the late 19th century. The 20th century's 10 warmest years all occurred in the last 15 years of the century. Of these, 1998 was the warmest year on record. The snow cover in the Northern Hemisphere and floating ice in the Arctic Ocean have decreased. Globally, sea level has risen 4-8 inches over the past century. Worldwide precipitation over land has increased by about one percent. The frequency of extreme rainfall events has increased throughout much of the United States.

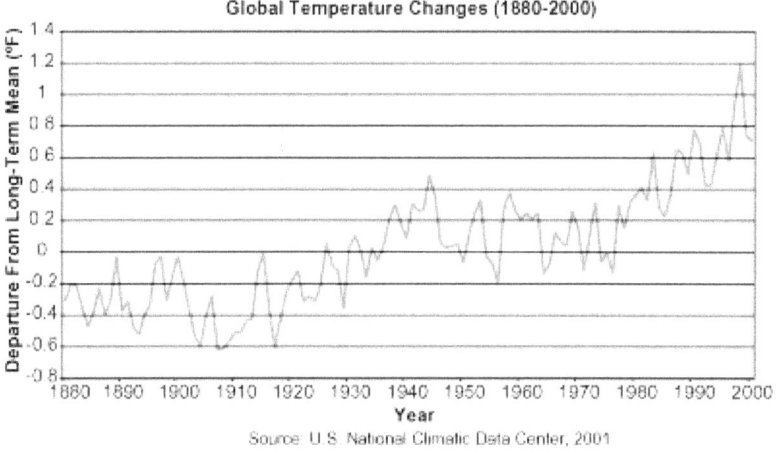

Increasing concentrations of greenhouse gases are likely to accelerate the rate of climate change. Scientists expect that the average global surface temperature could rise 1-4.5°F (0.6-2.5°C) in the next fifty years, and 2.2-10°F (1.4-5.8°C) in the next century, with significant regional variation. Evaporation will increase as the climate warms, which will increase average global precipitation. Soil moisture is likely to decline in many regions, and intense rainstorms are likely to become more frequent. Sea level is likely to rise two feet along most of the U.S. coast.

Calculations of climate change for specific areas are much less reliable than global calculations, and it is unclear whether regional climate will become more variable.

Scientists have identified that our health, agriculture, water resources, forests, wildlife and coastal areas are vulnerable to the changes that global warming may bring. But projecting what the exact impact will be over the 21st century remains very difficult. This is especially true when one asks how a local region will be affected.

Scientists are more confident about their projections for large-scale areas (e.g., global temperature and precipitation change, average sea level rise) and less confident about projections for small-scale areas (e.g., local temperature and precipitation changes, altered weather patterns, soil moisture changes). This is largely because the computer models used to forecast global climate change are still ill-equipped to simulate how things may change on smaller scales.

Some of the largest uncertainties are associated with events that pose the greatest risk to human societies. The IPCC cautions, "Complex systems, such as the climate system, can respond in non-linear ways and produce surprises." There is the possibility that a warmer world could lead to more frequent and intense storms, including hurricanes. Preliminary evidence suggests that, once hurricanes do form, they will be stronger if the oceans are warmer due to global warming. However, the jury is still out whether or not hurricanes and other storms will become more frequent.

More and more attention is being aimed at the possible link between El Niño events – the periodic warming of the equatorial Pacific Ocean – and global warming. Scientists are concerned that the accumulation of greenhouse gases could inject enough heat into Pacific waters such that El Niño events become more frequent and fierce. Here, too, research has not advanced far enough to provide conclusive statements about how global warming will affect El Niño scenarios.

LIVING WITH UNCERTAINTY

Like many pioneer fields of research, the current state of global warming science can't always provide definitive answers to our questions. There is certainty that human activities are rapidly adding greenhouse gases to the atmosphere, and that these gases tend to warm our planet. This is the basis for concern about global warming.

The fundamental scientific uncertainties are these: How much more warming will occur? How fast will this warming occur? And what are the potential adverse and beneficial effects? These uncertainties will be with us for some time, perhaps decades.

Global warming poses real risks. The exact nature of these risks remains uncertain. Ultimately, this is why we must use our best judgment – guided by the current state of science – to determine what the most appropriate response to global warming should be.

WHAT ARE GREENHOUSE GASES?

Some greenhouse gases occur naturally in the atmosphere, while others result from human activities. Naturally occurring greenhouse gases include water vapor, carbon dioxide, methane, nitrous oxide, and ozone. Certain human activities, however, add to the levels of most of these naturally occurring gases:

Carbon dioxide is released to the atmosphere when solid waste, fossil fuels (oil, natural gas, and coal), and wood and wood products are burned.

Methane is emitted during the production and transport of coal, natural gas, and oil. Methane emissions also result from the decomposition of organic wastes in municipal solid waste landfills, and the raising of livestock.

Nitrous oxide is emitted during agricultural and industrial activities, as well as during combustion of solid waste and fossil fuels.

Very powerful greenhouse gases that are not naturally occurring include *hydrofluorocarbons (HFCs), perfluorocarbons (PFCs), and sulfur hexafluoride (SF6)*, which are generated in a variety of industrial processes.

Each greenhouse gas differs in its ability to absorb heat in the atmosphere. HFCs and PFCs are the most heat-absorbent. Methane traps over 21 times more heat per molecule than carbon dioxide, and nitrous oxide absorbs 270 times more heat per molecule than carbon dioxide. Often, estimates of greenhouse gas emissions are presented in units of millions of metric tons of carbon equivalents (MMTCE), which weighs each gas by its GWP value, or Global Warming Potential.

WHAT ARE EMISSIONS INVENTORIES?

An emission inventory is an accounting of the amount of air pollutants discharged into the atmosphere. It is generally characterized by the following factors:
- the chemical or physical identity of the pollutants included,
- the geographic area covered,
- the institutional entities covered,
- the time period over which emissions are estimated, and
- the types of activities that cause emissions.

Emission inventories are developed for a variety of purposes. Inventories of natural and anthropogenic emissions are used by scientists as inputs to air quality models, by policy makers to develop strategies and policies or track progress of standards, and by facilities and regulatory agencies to establish compliance records with allowable emission rates. A well constructed inventory should include enough documentation and other data to allow readers to understand the underlying assumptions and to reconstruct the calculations for each of the estimates included.

WHAT ARE SINKS?

A sink is a reservoir that uptakes a chemical element or compound from another part of its cycle. For example, soil and trees tend to act as natural sinks for carbon – each year hundreds of billions of tons of carbon in the form of CO_2 are absorbed by oceans, soils, and trees.

POLLUTION

Pollution is the human-caused addition of any material or energy which results in unwanted alterations. There are three main impacts to pollution:

- physical
- chemical
- biological

ENVIRONMENTAL RISK ASSESSMENT

Risk analysis began at the EPA or Environmental Protection Agency. Originally formed to research cancer risks associated with chemicals, this agency now does much more. They are responsible for risk analysis that includes:

- hazard assessment – linking hazards to its effects.
- dose-response assessment – how much (chemical/pollution) for how long?
- exposure assessment – which human groups are already exposed to the chemical, the dose, the length of time, and how they got exposed.
- risk characterization – how many will die?

ACID RAIN

Acid rain is a broad term used to describe several ways that acids fall out of the atmosphere. A more precise term is acid deposition, which has two parts: wet and dry.

Wet deposition refers to acidic rain, fog, and snow. As this acidic water flows over and through the ground, it affects a variety of plants and animals. The strength of the effects depends on many factors, including how acidic the water is, the chemistry and buffering capacity of the soils involved, and the types of fish, trees, and other living things that rely on the water.

Dry deposition refers to acidic gases and particles. About half of the acidity in the atmosphere falls back to earth through dry deposition. The wind blows these acidic particles and gases onto buildings, cars, homes, and trees. Dry deposited gases and particles can also be washed from trees and other surfaces by rainstorms. When that happens, the runoff water adds those acids to the acid rain, making the combination more acidic than the falling rain alone.

Prevailing winds blow the compounds that cause both wet and dry acid deposition across state and national borders, and sometimes over hundreds of miles.

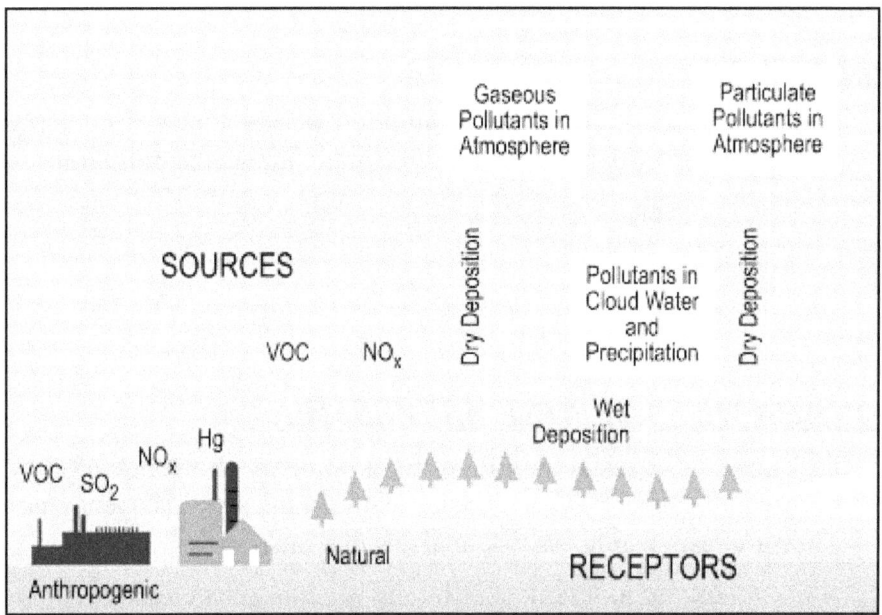

Scientists discovered, and have confirmed, that sulfur dioxide (SO2) and nitrogen oxides (NOx) are the primary causes of acid rain. In the US, about 2/3 of all SO2 and 1/4 of all NOx come from electric power generation that relies on burning fossil fuels like coal.

Acid rain occurs when these gases react in the atmosphere with water, oxygen, and other chemicals to form various acidic compounds. Sunlight increases the rate of most of these reactions. The result is a mild solution of sulfuric acid and nitric acid.

HOW DO WE MEASURE ACID RAIN?

Acid rain is measured using a scale called "pH." The lower a substance's pH, the more acidic it is. Pure water has a pH of 7.0. Normal rain is slightly acidic because carbon dioxide dissolves into it, so it has a pH of about 5.5. As of the year 2000, the most acidic rain falling in the US has a pH of about 4.3.

Acid rain's pH, and the chemicals that cause acid rain, are monitored by two networks, both supported by the EPA. Acidity in rain is measured by collecting samples of rain and measuring its pH. To find the distribution of rain acidity, weather conditions are monitored and rain samples are collected at sites all over the country. The areas of greatest acidity (lowest pH values) are located in the Northeastern United States. This pattern of high acidity is caused by the large number of cities, the dense population, and the concentration of power and industrial plants in the Northeast. In addition, the prevailing wind direction brings storms and pollution to the Northeast from the Midwest, and dust from the soil and rocks in the Northeastern United States is less likely to neutralize acidity in the rain.

WHAT ARE ACID RAIN'S EFFECTS?

Acid deposition has a variety of effects, including damage to forests and soils, fish and other living things, materials, and human health. Acid rain also reduces how far and how clearly we can see through the air, an effect called visibility reduction. Acid rain causes acidification of lakes and streams and contributes to damage of trees at high elevations (for example, red spruce trees above 2,000 feet) and many sensitive forest soils. In addition, acid rain accelerates the decay of building materials and paints, including irreplaceable buildings, statues, and sculptures that are part of our nation's cultural heritage. Prior to falling to the earth, SO2 and NOx gases and their particulate matter derivatives, sulfates and nitrates, contribute to visibility degradation and harm public health.

NONPOINT SOURCE POLLUTION

Nonpoint source (NPS) pollution, unlike pollution from industrial and sewage treatment plants, comes from many diffuse sources. NPS pollution is caused by rainfall or snow melt moving over and through the ground. As the runoff moves, it picks up and carries away natural and human-made pollutants, finally depositing them into lakes, rivers, wetlands, coastal waters, and even our underground sources of drinking water. These pollutants include:

- Excess fertilizers, herbicides, and insecticides from agricultural lands and residential areas;
- Oil, grease, and toxic chemicals from urban runoff and energy production;
- Sediment from improperly managed construction sites, crop and forest lands, and eroding stream banks;
- Salt from irrigation practices and acid drainage from abandoned mines;
- Bacteria and nutrients from livestock, pet wastes, and faulty septic systems;

Atmospheric deposition and hydromodification are also sources of nonpoint source pollution.

OZONE

Ozone is a gas that occurs both in the Earth's upper atmosphere and at ground level. Ozone can be "good" or "bad" for your health and the environment, depending on its location in the atmosphere.

HOW CAN OZONE BE BOTH GOOD AND BAD?

Ozone occurs in two layers of the atmosphere. The layer closest to the Earth's surface is the troposphere. Here, ground-level or "bad" ozone is an air pollutant that is harmful to breathe and it damages crops, trees and other vegetation. It is a main ingredient of urban smog. The troposphere generally extends to a level about six miles up, where it meets the second layer, the stratosphere. The stratosphere or "good" ozone layer extends upward from about 6 to 30 miles and protects life on Earth from the sun's harmful ultraviolet (UV) rays. Ozone (O3) is a form of oxygen which is important because it has the ability to absorb high energy radiation emitted by the sun, which can be harmful to people. The ozone layer of the atmosphere resides in the stratosphere. Because of this, temperature actually increases farther into the stratosphere.

The troposphere is the layer where weather occurs, meaning that there is a lot of vertical movement as water falls as precipitation, and later evaporates. This is quite different from the stratosphere which has virtually no vertical motion, so things remain there for long periods of time. Because there is no vertical motion within the stratosphere it is good that ozone is there. It can absorb the harmful radiation from the sun, without coming into contact with people. When there is ozone in the troposphere it can become dangerous. Since there is so much vertical motion it spreads throughout the layer, carrying the harmful radiation with it.

WHAT IS HAPPENING TO THE "GOOD" OZONE LAYER?

Ozone is produced naturally in the stratosphere. But this "good" ozone is gradually being destroyed by man-made chemicals referred to as ozone-depleting substances (ODS), including chlorofluorocarbons (CFCs), hydrochlorofluorocarbons (HCFCs), halons, methyl bromide, carbon tetrachloride, and methyl chloroform. These substances were formerly used and sometimes still are used in coolants, foaming agents, fire extinguishers, solvents, pesticides, and aerosol propellants. Once released into the air these ozone-depleting substances degrade very slowly. In fact, they can remain intact for years as they move through the troposphere until they reach the stratosphere. There they are broken down by the intensity of the sun's UV rays and release chlorine and bromine molecules, which destroy the "good" ozone. Scientists estimate that one chlorine atom can destroy 100,000 "good" ozone molecules.

Even though we have reduced or eliminated the use of many ODSs, their use in the past can still affect the protective ozone layer. Research indicates that depletion of the "good" ozone layer is being reduced worldwide. The thinning of the protective ozone layer can be observed using satellite measurements, particularly over the Polar Regions.

HOW DOES THE DEPLETION OF "GOOD" OZONE AFFECT HUMAN HEALTH AND THE ENVIRONMENT?

Ozone depletion can cause increased amounts of UV radiation to reach the Earth which can lead to more cases of skin cancer, cataracts, and impaired immune systems. Overexposure to UV is believed to be contributing to the increase in melanoma, the most fatal of all skin cancers. Since 1990, the risk of developing melanoma has more than doubled.

UV can also damage sensitive crops, such as soybeans, and reduce crop yields. Some scientists suggest that marine phytoplankton, which are the base of the ocean food chain, are already under stress from UV radiation. This stress could have adverse consequences for human food supplies from the oceans.

WHAT IS BEING DONE ABOUT THE DEPLETION OF "GOOD" OZONE?

The United States, along with over 180 other countries, recognized the threats posed by ozone depletion and in 1987 adopted a treaty called the Montreal Protocol to phase out the production and use of ozone-depleting substances.

The EPA has established regulations to phase out ozone-depleting chemicals in the United States. Warning labels must be placed on all products containing CFCs or similar substances and nonessential uses of ozone-depleting products are prohibited. Releases into the air of refrigerants used in car and home air conditioning units and appliances are also prohibited. Some substitutes to ozone-depleting products have been produced and others are being developed. If the United States and other countries stop producing ozone-depleting substances, natural ozone production should return the ozone layer to normal levels by about 2050.

WHAT CAUSES "BAD" OZONE?

Ground-level or "bad" ozone is not emitted directly into the air, but is created by chemical reactions between oxides of nitrogen (NOx) and volatile organic compounds (VOC) in the presence of sunlight. Emissions from industrial facilities and electric utilities, motor vehicle exhaust, gasoline vapors, and chemical solvents are some of the major sources of NOx and VOC.

At ground level, ozone is a harmful pollutant. Ozone pollution is a concern during the summer months because strong sunlight and hot weather result in harmful ozone concentrations in the air we breathe. Many urban and suburban areas throughout the United States have high levels of "bad" ozone. But many rural areas of the country are also subject to high ozone levels as winds carry emissions hundreds of miles away from their original sources.

HOW DOES "BAD" OZONE AFFECT HUMAN HEALTH AND THE ENVIRONMENT?

Breathing ozone can trigger a variety of health problems including chest pain, coughing, throat irritation, and congestion. It can worsen bronchitis, emphysema, and asthma. "Bad" ozone also can reduce lung function and inflame the lining of the lungs. Repeated exposure may permanently scar lung tissue.

Healthy people also experience difficulty breathing when exposed to ozone pollution. Because ozone forms in hot weather, anyone who spends time outdoors in the summer may be affected, particularly children, outdoor workers and people exercising. Millions of Americans live in areas where the national ozone health standards are exceeded.

Ground-level or "bad" ozone also damages vegetation and ecosystems. It leads to reduced agricultural crop and commercial forest yields, reduced growth and survivability of tree seedlings, and increased susceptibility to diseases, pests and other stresses such as harsh weather. In the United States alone, ground-level ozone is responsible for an estimated $500 million in reduced crop production each year. Ground-level ozone also damages the foliage of trees and other plants, affecting the landscape of cities, national parks and forests, and recreation areas.

WHAT IS BEING DONE ABOUT "BAD" OZONE?

Under the Clean Air Act, the EPA has set protective health-based standards for ozone in the air we breathe. The EPA, state, and cities have instituted a variety of multi-faceted programs to meet these health-based standards. Throughout the country, additional programs are being put into place to cut NOx and VOC emissions from vehicles, industrial facilities, and electric utilities. Programs are also aimed at reducing pollution by reformulating fuels and consumer/commercial products, such as paints and chemical solvents that contain VOC. Voluntary programs also encourage communities to adopt practices, such as carpooling, to reduce harmful emissions.

HIGH-ALTITUDE "GOOD" OZONE

- Protect yourself against sunburn. When the UV Index is "high" or "very high", limit outdoor activities between 10 am and 4 pm, when the sun is most intense.

Environmental Science

Twenty minutes before going outside, liberally apply a broad-spectrum sunscreen with a Sun Protection Factor (SPF) of at least 15. Reapply every two hours or after swimming or sweating. For UV Index forecasts, check local media reports or visit: www.epa.gov/sunwise/uvindex.html

- Use approved refrigerants in air conditioning and refrigeration equipment. Make sure technicians that work on your car or home air conditioners or refrigerator are certified to recover the refrigerant. Repair leaky air conditioning units before refilling them.

GROUND-LEVEL "BAD" OZONE

- Check the air quality forecast in your area. At times when the Air Quality Index (AQI) is forecast to be unhealthy, limit physical exertion outdoors. In many places, ozone peaks in mid-afternoon to early evening. Change the time of day of strenuous outdoor activity to avoid these hours, or reduce the intensity of the activity. For AQI forecasts, check your local media reports or visit: www.epa.gov/airnow

- Help your local electric utilities reduce ozone air pollution by conserving energy at home and the office. Consider setting your thermostat a little higher in the summer. Participate in your local utilities' load-sharing and energy conservation programs.

- Reduce air pollution from cars, trucks, gas-powered lawn and garden equipment, boats and other engines by keeping equipment properly tuned and maintained. During the summer, fill your gas tank during the cooler evening hours and be careful not to spill gasoline. Reduce driving, carpool, use public transportation, walk, or bicycle to reduce ozone pollution, especially on hot summer days.

- Use household and garden chemicals wisely. Use low VOC paints and solvents. And be sure to read labels for proper use and disposal.

EUTROPHICATION

Eutrophication is when so many nutrients are brought via a river so that phytoplankton (algae) grow abundantly on the surface and take up the light such that other plants on the bottom do not receive enough light through the water to perform photosynthesis. Normally, bacteria decompose things such as dead fish, which releases nutrients for the algae to feed on. The algae are then eaten by zooplankton, which are eaten by fish which die and are decomposed, completing the cycle.

Over time bodies of water become subject to a process called eutrophication. This occurs when the algae grows to the surface of the water and covers it. The algae underneath can then no longer receive the necessary sunlight for photosynthesis and die off. The bacteria begin to decompose the algae. Because of the abundance of algae, large amounts of oxygen are removed from the water during the decomposition process.

Because the plants are not creating oxygen in the water, fish and shellfish die. The water becomes **turbid,** meaning murky or dark from sediment and algae. This happened to Chesapeake Bay in the 1980s.

Lower levels of oxygen mean that any water animals die, creating even greater oxygen consumption by the bacteria. Eventually, there is not enough oxygen to support the decomposition, and foul smelling waste begins to accumulate. This process occurs naturally over thousands of years and when it does it is called natural eutrophication. However, humankind has accelerated the process so that it has begun occurring in time frames as little as a few decades. One way this occurs is that algae growth is stimulated by nutrients from pollution, allowing it to grow faster than the zooplankton can consume it. When eutrophication occurs due to humankind it is called cultural eutrophication.

DEFORESTATION AND DESERTIFICATION

Deforestation occurs when the removal of the forest by cutting and burning is done to make room for farm land, houses, roads or other needs. Basically, it is the destruction of forest land. Remember our example from the section on trophic levels.

Desertification is the creation or spread of the desert to places that were not previously desert.

Ecological Concepts

ENVIRONMENTAL SCIENCE

Environmental science is the science of studying effects that humans have on the environment. Another term for environmental science is ecology but ecology is more specific to how organisms relate and live within their environment. This cause-and-effect relationship is studied to show how the world works, how natural resources are created and regenerated, and how this affects our daily lives. Life started out simply enough on this planet, but now complex issues such as pollution and the ozone layer require discussion and solutions.

ECOSYSTEMS

There are three parts to the layer around the earth called the **biosphere**. The air is the atmosphere, the water is the hydrosphere and the minerals are the lithosphere. An ecosystem is a group of specific species of plants, animals and microbes that interact with each other and their environment, which includes temperature, seasons, moisture, etc.

BIOMES AND TERRESTRIAL COMMUNITIES

There are many different types of **biomes**. A biome is a major, classified, recognized community having well-recognized plant and animal life. Here is a list of the most common ones:

- Desert – Few plants and animals make their home here. There is little or no rainfall; less than 10 inches a year makes an area a desert.
- Deep Sea – The deep sea ecosystems are unlike any others, the main reason being that it has developed in an area void of sunlight. Most ecosystems are dependent on the sun to survive. Organisms on the ocean floor take their energy directly from the earth through hydrothermal vents. Hydrothermal vents are essentially geysers found on the ocean floor. They send out geothermally heated water which the organisms thrive on.
- Coniferous Forest – This evergreen forest begins where tundra gives way to trees. This area is very cold in the winter time and pleasant during the summer.
- Grasslands – These areas are home to grazing animals. Grasslands grow where there is not enough moisture for trees.
- Deciduous Forest – This forest "turns" with the seasons; trees lose their leaves and there is snow. This biome experiences a full four seasons.
- Steppe – This is a large, flat area of land. Steppes are generally covered with short grasses less than one foot tall and receive 10 to 20 inches of rain a year. To put that in perspective, steppes receive more rain than deserts, but less than prairies. Steppes are mostly used to grow wheat or graze livestock.
- Tropical Rain Forest – These are found near the equator, are very hot and humid with a variety of different plants, animals and insects living together.
- Temperate Rain Forest – This a more temperate rain forest, and is slightly cooler than the tropical rain forest with less diversity of plant life, although it is still humid.
- Tundra – Tundra is found in the icy zones in the arctic. They have a very short growing period and no trees. Winter temperatures can be as cold as -70 Fahrenheit. It includes a thick layer of permafrost, a permanently frozen sub layer of soil.
- Aquatic – Water takes up more than 75% of the world's surface. There are many different types of aquatic biomes including salt water, fresh water and estuaries which are where the freshwater rivers or streams mix with the ocean.

- Savannah – Tropical grassland found in Africa, which includes a small amount of trees and large game.
- Taiga – This is the largest land biome. Cold in the winter and warm in the summer, it includes a large part of Canada and is home to moose and grizzly bear.
- Veldt – A veldt is similar to a steppe, but is used to describe the large, open grasslands in southern Africa.

The single greatest factor in determining what area a biome falls into is based on how much rainfall it experiences in a year.

ROLES OF ORGANISMS AND FOOD CHAIN

Organisms are broken up into three main categories: producers, consumers or decomposers (sometimes called detritus feeders).

Producers are mostly green plants that use energy from the sun to create food through photosynthesis. Consumers are animals that eat or consume anything. An example of a consumer would be a rabbit eating grass. The grass is a producer, the rabbit a consumer. If a fox were to eat the rabbit, the fox would be a consumer, the rabbit would still be a consumer and the grass would be a producer. An example of a decomposer would be the bugs, bacteria and fungi that break down the remains of the rabbit that the fox didn't eat. If a hyena were to eat a fox, that hyena would be called a tertiary consumer. The rabbit would be the primary consumer, the fox the secondary consumer, etc.

This is an example of a food chain. Each animal or plant that is eaten represents a link in the chain. A food web is simply a collection of overlapping food chains. For example, in our plant-rabbit-fox-hyena scenario, you could also have a plant-rabbit-fox-human chain. These two chains together form a food web.

Organic substances are plant and animal products. Inorganic substances include water, minerals, rocks, soil, gasses, etc. The exercise of photosynthesis for example takes an inorganic substance (light, and gas) to create plants, which are organic substances. When a plant dies, it is decomposed, returning again to inorganic compounds.

BIOGEOCHEMICAL CYCLING

Biogeochemical cycling is a term that represents the cycling of natural resources such as water, nitrogen, sulfur and carbon. The **hydrologic cycle** is the cycle of water. Water covers over 75% of the earth. However, that is mostly salt water, which has little use to humans that need a large amount of water for food preparation, consumption, etc. Scientists are still looking for a way to purify salt water that is cost effective to use.

Until that time, we need to be conscious of the amount of water we use and make sure it doesn't go to waste.

Water is created by plants through transpiration, which releases it into the atmosphere later to return as rain, ground water, etc. Water also carries with it sediment and minerals when evaporated. Rivers also deposit sediment in the ocean or lakes to which they connect.

Nitrogen makes up about 80% of the atmosphere. Nitrogen compounds are then attached to soil. Nitrogen is used by plants to create food. Nitrogen returns to its gas form when a plant is eaten or dies. Human interactions with the environment sometimes restrict the nitrogen as it tries to return to the atmosphere, resulting in smog and other problems.

Organisms need a low amount of sulfur to be healthy. Sulfur starts as gas and is transported through the earth via rain or just falling down naturally. Sulfur is returned to its gas form almost the same way as nitrogen and can cause problems with erosion, acid rain, etc.

Carbon is the key element to life on earth. All living things are composed of carbon. Plants use carbon dioxide in photosynthesis to create sugars and excrete oxygen. Carbon dioxide can become trapped and be transformed into pockets of coal or petroleum. Coal when combined with extreme pressure results in diamonds.

Sulfur is an essential element for living things. Sulfur occurs naturally in volcanic springs and hot thermal vents. Like nitrogen and water it moves through a biogeochemical cycle where it moves through the ecosystem from the ground through decomposition, to the atmosphere, where it mixes with rain and other sulfur in the atmosphere to create acid rain.

Phosphorous is an important nutrient for plants and animals. It is present in DNA molecules. It is also present in the cells that form bones and teeth. Phosphorous is never in the air in a gaseous state. At room temperature, it is a liquid. In the air, it is actually very small dust particles. Phosphorous is the slowest of the biogeochemical cycles. Phosphorous is found in rocks and in the ocean. Phosphorous is released through rocks weathering and will dissolve in water and soil. This leaves very small amounts of phosphorous in the soil. Because phosphorous encourages plant growth, farmers give their plants phosphorous fertilizers. Animals and humans get phosphorous by eating plants that have absorbed it from the soil. When the animals die and decompose, the phosphorous is returned back to the soil and the cycle begins again.

WASTEWATER TREATMENT

Most cities currently treat their **wastewater,** which is the water the goes down the sink, bathtub, gutter, drain and toilet. This water is taken to a plant where it is treated so it can be reused by the environment and society. The preliminary treatment involves taking out the trash from the water.

A screen shaped by bars, screen raw wastewater (called influent) as it enters the treatment facility to remove large debris like trash, paper, and weeds. After screening, wastewater is pumped into aerated grit chambers that remove sand and gravel. The debris and grit removed during this process are trucked to a landfill. Then the primary treatment begins. Wastewater settles in long tanks called primary sedimentation tanks. Heavy material sinks to the bottom (as sludge), and light material floats to the top (as scum). Skimmers remove scum from the surface of the water and scrapers remove sludge from the tank bottom.

Both are then sent onto the solids handling process. At this point anything that could have settled out has. The treated water, now called primary effluent, flows to the flow diversion structure.

The secondary treatment is when primary effluent is pumped to aeration tanks where oxygen is added to encourage growth of useful bacteria naturally present in the wastewater. Bacteria is eating the harmful elements in the water, cleaning it for us.

In the process, they produce more bacteria. The wastewater then goes to secondary clarifiers, large round sedimentation tanks where bacteria settle to the bottom of the tank as secondary sludge. Most (90 percent) of secondary sludge goes back to the aeration tanks to process ("eat") more organic material; the rest goes to the solids handling process. The remaining water—secondary effluent— leaves the clarifiers at least 85 percent cleaner than when it entered the facility. The water is then disinfected by being chlorinated, destroying most remaining pathogens, or disease-causing bacteria.

The final effluent is dechlorinated before it is released into the secondary water system or back into the wild.

TROPHIC LEVELS

Trophic levels are just another part of the food chain. Basically, **think of trophic levels as a pyramid**. At the bottom, you have the primary producers, followed by the primary consumers, secondary consumers and at the top of the pyramid you have the final consumers. Let's add some round numbers to it. It would take 1000 grass plants to support 10 rabbits. It takes 5 rabbits to support one fox. It takes 10 foxes to support one hyena. Do you see where we've fallen off track? It takes a HUGE amount of primary producers to support one final consumer.

Here's another example: a cow must eat a great deal of grain to become big and large enough for a farmer to take it to market to become beef via steak or hamburger. There is a great total cost for eating meat. The amount of plants the animal requires to become meat is very large. Developing countries in South America often clear their rainforest ground to raise beef because it pays quite a bit of money in their market. This is money that they will in turn use to buy food to feed their own family. In reality, most would be better off growing their own vegetables for their family because it would use much less of their land and would protect their ecosystem.

In trophic levels, **biomagnification** can occur. Biomagnification is when something that cannot be degraded is passed through the food chain from one organism to another until the final organism has accumulated a very large portion of the contaminant.

For example, a zooplankton may have a large amount of DDT. The next thing in the food chain to eat it will also acquire the DDT. So, the rainbow trout now has the same exposure to the DDT it had before, let's put a number on it of 5. By consuming the zooplankton, it now has a level of 7. The next thing in the food chain, a larger fish or bird will then eat the rainbow trout and will acquire the level of DDT of what it ate. This is dangerous because the larger amount of the chemical, the more harmful effect. This chemical is passed on because it is not easily broken down like lead is not easily broken down.

The process of biomagnification shows how even small amounts of dangerous substances in an environment can become dangerous to organisms higher up on the food chain. Until levels of the chemicals or metals reach a point where they begin causing problems, they go unnoticed. However, by the time symptoms begin showing, it is usually too late to do anything about it.

Biomagnification is generally used when referring to heavy metals which tend to be highly fat soluble, but not particularly water soluble. Heavy metals initially enter the body while dissolved in water, and upon coming into contact with lipid membranes (which are fatty compounds) the metals enter the lipids and remain there, this process is called bioaccumulation. When biomagnification then occurs, the metals continue to pass through fat tissue.

Bioaccumulation is when substances such as heavy metals build up in an organism's fatty compounds (such as lipids). Because of bioaccumulation, when that organism is consumed, biomagnification occurs. The main difference between the two is that bioaccumulation generally describes an organism accumulating toxins from water or the environment. Biomagnification, on the other hand, describes the process whereby the concentrations of a toxin increases through consuming another organism.

ENERGY FLOW

Energy for all systems and food chains begins with the sun. The sun provides the light for the plants to create photosynthesis, which creates food for the rabbit, which creates food for the fox, etc. When a plant or animal is consumed, the energy of that item is released. For example, the sun transfers energy to the plant which is eaten by the rabbit. The rabbit is consuming or releasing the energy of the plant.

BIODIVERSITY

Not all plants are producers; there are others such as fungi, mushrooms, molds, and Indian pipe plant. There are two ways to classify anything in the biosphere: heterotrophs and autotrophs. Autotrophs can create the food and nutrients that they need to survive. Examples of autotrophs are plants like grass or trees. They can produce what they need to survive. Heterotrophs however do not. They need to consume autotrophs to get their food and energy. So, a grass plant is a producer and is also an autotroph. A rabbit is a heterotroph and a consumer.

There are also three types of consumers: carnivores, herbivores and omnivores. Carnivores are animals that only eat meat (other animals). Herbivores are animals that eat only plants. Omnivores are consumers that eat both plants and animals, like most humans.

When an animal attacks and kills another to consume it, the animal consuming the food is called the predator. He will hunt the prey (food). Parasites are organisms that can be plants or animals that feed on or take advantage of their host. The word parasite denotes a negative effect for the host. A symbiotic relationship is when both the host and the parasite benefit from the relationship as referred to as a mutualism. For example, clown fish (think Nemo) are immune to the tentacles of sea anemones. So the clown fish are able to feed on and around the sea anemones while receiving their protection from other predators. The anemones benefit by being cleaned (think gross fish tank).

POPULATION

Each species in an ecosystem is a population. A group of deer is a population, a group of penguins is a population, etc. A population has to be an interbreeding and reproducing group. A population is effected by a birth rate and a death rate. Carrying capacity is the amount (population) of a certain animal that can be supported in a specific area, long term. For example, the carrying capacity for a one-acre field of grass may be 23 rabbits.

BIRTH RATE AND DEATH RATE

A **birth rate** is calculated by dividing the number of live births in a population in a year by the midyear resident population. For census years, rates are based on unrounded census counts of the resident population, as of April 1st. Birth rates are expressed as the number of live births per 1,000 population. The rate may be restricted to births to women of specific age, race, marital status, or geographic location (specific rate), or it may be related to the entire population (crude rate).

A **death rate** is calculated by dividing the number of deaths in a population in a year by the midyear resident population. For census years, rates are based on unrounded census counts of the resident population, as of April 1st. Death rates are expressed as the number of deaths per 100,000 population. The rate may be restricted to deaths in specific age, race, sex, or geographic groups or from specific causes of death (specific rate) or it may be related to the entire population (crude rate).

A **fetal death rate** is the number of fetal deaths with stated or presumed gestation of 20 weeks or more divided by the sum of live births plus fetal deaths, per 1,000 live births plus fetal deaths.

An **infant mortality rate** is based on period files calculated by dividing the number of infant deaths during a calendar year by the number of live births reported in the same year. It is expressed as the number of infant deaths per 1,000 live births.

A **neonatal mortality rate** is the number of deaths of children under 28 days of age, per 1,000 live births.

A **post neonatal mortality rate** is the number of deaths of children that occur between 28 days and 365 days after birth, per 1,000 live births.

Birth cohort infant mortality rates are based on linked birth and infant death files. In contrast to period rates in which the births and infant deaths occur in the same period or calendar year, infant deaths comprising the numerator of a birth cohort rate may have occurred in the same year as, or in the year following the year of birth. The birth cohort infant mortality rate is expressed as the number of infant deaths per 1,000 live births.

Maternal mortality rate is defined as the number of maternal deaths per 100,000 live births. The maternal mortality rate is a measure of the likelihood that a pregnant woman will die from maternal causes. The number of live births used in the denominator is a proxy for the population of pregnant women who are at risk of a maternal death.

Fertility rate is the total number of live births, regardless of age of mother, per 1,000 women of reproductive age, 15-44 years.

Total fertility rate (TFR) shows the potential impact of current fertility patterns on reproduction, that is, completed family size. The TFR indicates the average number of births to a hypothetical cohort of 1,000 women, if they experienced throughout their childbearing years the age-specific birth rates observed in a given year. Because it is based on age-specific birth rates, the TFR is not affected by changes over time in the age composition of a population and can be used to compare populations over time or between different groups.

Gross reproduction rate (GRR) represents the average number of daughters born to a hypothetical cohort of 1,000 women if they experienced the age-specific birth rates observed in a given year throughout their childbearing years and if none of the cohort was to die during her childbearing years. The GRR is similar to the total fertility rate (TFR) except that it measures only female births, since reproduction is largely dependent on the number of females in a given population. Moreover, like the TFR, the GRR is age adjusted and thus rates can be compared over time or between different groups.

BIODIVERSITY AND SUSTAINABILITY

There are four main principles to ecosystem sustainability. Ecosystems must:

1. Dispose of wastes and replenish nutrients by recycling
2. Use sunlight as their only source of energy
3. Maintain consumer populations
4. Maintain biodiversity

For a balanced ecosystem, there must be a balance held between consumers and predators or other elements. For example, in one situation there are 100 deer living in the hills outside the city. There are no natural predators in the area and hunting is not allowed. Through a few seasons, the population of deer will grow and multiply until there is not enough food to support the deer population in the hills. Now there are 2000 deer. The deer then will travel outside their normal habitat to find food, resulting in the deer coming into the city. Deer are killed by cars and by consuming food from residences. The local population is concerned and leaves spoiled fruit and other food outside for the deer. The deer eat until their stomachs are full but they cannot process the foreign food or the food does not hold the nutrients that they need so they are dying. That winter most of the deer die, leaving only 50 or so who retreat to the hills above the city. While also being a true story, this example shows you what happens when there is not a natural balance to the ecosystem. Another way that people have tried to solve similar problems is by instituting hunting to keep the population down and making sure it is not depleted too greatly by only issuing a few licenses.

EVOLUTION

Evolution is the theory that all organisms change and adapt to their surroundings over time. Through time, animals gain the traits they need to survive and perpetuate. For example, the finches that Darwin studied each had a different shape of beak. The reason for this was determined that each beak shape helped the bird get a certain type of food or nut that it would otherwise be unable to eat.

AGRICULTURAL AND INDUSTRIAL REVOLUTIONS

In addition to the biological steps in evolution there were also impacts on the social behaviors of humans. Humans would consume plants, berries, seeds, nuts and animals that they could catch and kill. It was at this time that humans were a hunting and gathering society. This method of getting food made it impossible for humans to stay in one place for a given amount of time without depleting the resources of the area. In time, humans began cultivating and farming, one of the most significant developments in agriculture and in the human race.

Once farming began, early populations of humans began to increase. Because less time was taken up in procuring food, more stable shelters could be created and new crafts could be developed and honed. There was also the development of crops. Farmers were weather-dependent for food as well as dependent on intense physical labor. People also began building permanent buildings to live in. They created a sense of community and established villages and towns.

As towns grew larger and larger, people had to begin to deal with the problems of having a large amount of people living in a small area. Decisions had to be made about water, waste removal, etc.

Technology necessary for agriculture took on new developments. The wheel and the plow were two of the greatest inventions that furthered farming.

Until the industrial revolution, most of the world's population was rural. The Industrial Revolution involved inventions such as the steam engine, railroads, and steamships. The industrial revolution happened when people began to use machinery to help with farming and manufacturing.

By 1762, England already had machinery in manufacturing plants, as well as a staff of 600 workers. Electric power is another invention with huge consequences for the world. It extended the working day as well as provided electricity to the manufacturing plants.

Advances in transportation and the automobile made huge impacts, as did the tool of global communication, the telephone.

SUCCESSION ON LAND AND IN FRESHWATER

Succession is basically one organism invading or taking over a given area. For example, a barren area of rocks would experience **primary succession** when moss begins to grow on it. Moss is one of the few things that can live in such an inhospitable environment as bare rock. **Secondary succession** occurs when an area such as a farm field is abandoned and the area returns to its natural state. Crab grass is usually one of the first plants to grow in that type of area followed by tall grass and weeds over the next three years.

From years three to ten, pines and other trees will begin growing. From years ten to thirty, it will become a pine forest followed by hardwood trees growing in the next forty years. Natural disasters such as fire will remove all the new plant life from this area, which will begin the cycle anew with the crab grass.

Aquatic succession is when lakes or ponds gradually convert into forest ecosystems. Rivers and streams carry sediment to lakes. The lake bottom is gradually built up over years, making the lake more and more shallow, until it becomes dry land. This also occurs with ponds.

Over time, if a pond remains untouched, it will eventually turn into land. This process occurs over hundreds of years, and is called pond succession. First, algae and other submerged plants begin to develop. These are called pond pioneers. Over time, animals begin to inhabit the pond as well, and debris begins to build up. As time goes on, plants die, fall to the bottom of the pond and decompose. Layers build upon each other and the pond begins to fill in. Over time the pond becomes a marsh, and eventually the marsh dries out and becomes land.

 Environmental Management and Conservation

RENEWABLE AND NONRENEWABLE RESOURCES

Renewable resources are resources that can be renewed or replenished as fast as or faster than they are used. Examples of renewable resources are solar power, wind and geothermal resources. Also renewable, but not as fast, are items such as plant growth, water, and animals. These items can be renewed and reproduced but that process takes a longer amount of time.

Nonrenewable resources cannot easily be replaced because of the severe amount of time that it takes to create them – or simply that human consumption far outweighs the speed at which they can be reproduced. Some examples of nonrenewable resources are coal, oil and various metals.

THE GREEN REVOLUTION

The Green Revolution began with a group of scientists headed by Norman Borlaug that were sent to Mexico to try and improve the yield of the crops there. Basically, the Mexican farmers were not able to produce enough wheat to feed the entire country, making it necessary to import wheat. Borlaug along with his team created a hybrid wheat, using the existing Mexican wheat with a different wheat. This was a more hardy producing wheat and resulted in a huge success. Farmers were able to get much more out of the same amount of plants and within about 10 years, Mexico was able to stop importing and begin exporting wheat. Borlaug later received the Nobel Peace prize for his work.

Similar techniques were used in other countries such as India, where a new breed of wheat was introduced. Soon, many third world countries had their famine problems under control. Although it has had a remarkable impact, the Green Revolution is not the answer to all problems, because of the following:

- Many of the most heavily populated countries are already using this technology and have reached a plateau in their production.
- This does not work without irrigation in drought-prone areas and requires fertilizer, pesticides and mechanical labor, which are hard to come by in most third world countries.
- Green Revolution agriculture benefits larger land owners. Because of their great success, the process can displace smaller farmers who must leave to find a new trade or become unemployed.
- Important African food crops are not commonly used in the developed world so many farmers of such products have not benefited from Green Revolution technology.

North America has become what is called the world's "breadbasket" because of the great amount of exportable grains.

PESTICIDES AND PEST CONTROL

Pesticides and pest control are important because pests destroy approximately 37% of potential agricultural products. Pests include insects, plant pathogens and weeds, not to mention animals that feed on plants such as mice, birds, etc. Animals that attack, injure or kill livestock or other farm animals are also known as pests, which would be animals such as wolves, coyotes, etc. Think of a pest as any insect or animal that negatively impacts growing or producing food.

Herbicides are chemicals that kill plants. Pesticides are chemicals that kill animals and insects that are determined to be pests. Crop dusting, spraying chemicals on plants from a low flying airplane, is a basic technique to rid crops of insects.

Originally, many chemicals such as lead, arsenic and mercury were used to kill insects on plants. Because those stay around in the soil and have a poisoning effect on humans, these are known as first-generation pathogens. Because the first-generation pesticides became not as effective as insects began to adapt, second generation pesticides were created.

DDT was created and instituted in the 1930s. It was so successful because it killed a large variety of insects, was cheap to produce, and seemed to have little effect on humans and mammals. During WWII DDT was used to control body lice and control the number of mosquitoes, helping to curb malaria. The inventor of DDT also won the Novel Prize in 1948. DDT was a remarkable breakthrough in helping farmers combat bugs and other pests.

The book *Silent Spring* by Rachel Carson later revealed her scientific findings about the horrific effects of DDT. This is considered the ground breaking of the environmental movement. DDT was later and is still banned by the EPA.

SOIL CONSERVATION

Soil is made up from bits of rocks, dirt, dead leaves, etc. Soil has pores which are little cracks that let in air and water. Soil is a natural body comprised of solids (minerals and organic matter), liquid, and gases that occurs on the land surface, occupies space, and is characterized by one or both of the following: horizons, or layers, that are distinguishable from the initial material as a result of additions, losses, transfers, and transformations of energy and matter or the ability to support rooted plants in a natural environment.

The upper limit of soil is the boundary between soil and air, shallow water, live plants, or plant materials that have not begun to decompose. Areas are not considered to have soil if the surface is permanently covered by water too deep (typically more than 2.5 meters) for the growth of rooted plants.

The lower boundary that separates soil from the nonsoil underneath is most difficult to define. Soil consists of horizons near the earth's surface that, in contrast to the underlying parent material, have been altered by the interactions of climate, relief, and living organisms over time. Commonly, soil grades at its lower boundary to hard rock or to earthy materials virtually devoid of animals, roots, or other marks of biological activity. For purposes of classification, the lower boundary of soil is arbitrarily set at 200 cm.

Erosion is when the elements like wind and water erode away land. Animals as well as humans contribute to erosion, like on beach cliffs. Large amounts of water can also cut through the soil, making their own channel through the path of least resistance and carrying the sediment away. Recent heavy rains in San Diego, California are another example of erosion. Houses have slipped off hills as the dirt under them was carried away by the torrential rain.

Farmers have used strip cropping or strip farming as a way to utilize land for farming. This is when the farmer has a strip of land that is on a slope that it too long or too steep to support regular crops. Farmers will grow several mixed crops close together such as hay and wheat in between corn or soybeans. This helps prevent soil erosion and gives the farmer more room to cultivate. Strip cropping helps keep the water in the crops. This allows the water to sink into the ground and have nutrients deposited there that normally would have washed away without the intervention of the crops.

Contour cropping is a similar strategy to prevent erosion but instead of planting crops on the slope, groups of crops are sown on the contours across the slopes. This changes the natural path of water run-off and slows any remaining run off.

LAND USE

In a certain amount of area, all the water that drains into that area is called the watershed. The watershed can be in a forested area where the water from rain soaks into the ground and becomes part of the ground water, which contributes to the watershed. When an area is suffering from deforestation, the water compacts the soil, making the water unable to soak down into the ground and causing erosion. Dams and reservoirs are built to capture water.

Runoff is the water that does not go through normal channels. Runoff may happen when a channel overflows and runs across the ground. Because water picks up most things it comes across, it will have a variety of pollutants in it and will spread them.

AIR POLLUTION

When people think about air pollution, they usually think about smog, acid rain, CFC's, and other forms of outdoor air pollution. But did you know that air pollution also can exist inside homes and other buildings? It can, and every year, the health of many people is affected by chemical substances present in the air within buildings.

A great deal of research on pollution is being conducted at laboratories and universities. The goals of the research are to find solutions and to educate the public about the problem.

Air supplies us with oxygen which is essential for our bodies to live. Air is 99.9% nitrogen, oxygen, water vapor and inert gases. Human activities can release substances into the air, some of which can cause problems for humans, plants, and animals.

There are several main types of pollution and well-known effects of pollution that are commonly discussed. These include smog, acid rain, the greenhouse effect, and "holes" in the ozone layer. Each of these problems has serious implications for our health and well-being as well as for the whole environment.

One type of air pollution is the release of particles into the air from burning fuel for energy. Diesel smoke is a good example of this particulate matter. The particles are very small pieces of matter measuring about 2.5 microns or about .0001 inches. This type of pollution is sometimes referred to as "black carbon" pollution. The exhaust from burning fuels in automobiles, homes, and industries is a major source of pollution in the air. Some authorities believe that even the burning of wood and charcoal in fireplaces and barbecues can release significant quantities of soot into the air.

Another type of pollution is the release of noxious gases, such as sulfur dioxide, carbon monoxide, nitrogen oxides, and chemical vapors. These can take part in further chemical reactions once they are in the atmosphere, forming smog and acid rain.

Pollution also needs to be considered inside our homes, offices, and schools. Some of these pollutants can be created by indoor activities such as smoking and cooking. In the United States, we spend about 80-90% of our time inside buildings, and so our exposure to harmful indoor pollutants can be serious. It is therefore important to consider both indoor and outdoor air pollution.

Smog is a type of large-scale outdoor pollution. It is caused by chemical reactions between pollutants derived from different sources, primarily automobile exhaust and industrial emissions. Cities are often centers of these activities, and many suffer from the effects of smog, especially during the warm months of the year.

For each city, the exact causes of pollution may be different. Depending on the geographical location, temperature, wind and weather factors, pollution is dispersed differently. However, sometimes this does not happen and the pollution can build up to dangerous levels. A temperature inversion occurs when air close to the earth is cooler than the air above it. Under these conditions the pollution cannot rise and be dispersed. Cities surrounded by mountains also experience trapping of pollution. Inversion can happen in any season. Winter inversions are likely to cause particulate and carbon monoxide pollution. Summer inversions are more likely to create smog.

For the average person, driving their car is the most air polluting activity that they do. When a car burns fuel, dangerous gases are released into the air. These gases are also called greenhouse gases, and are often blamed for the global climate change phenomenon. Although essentially all fossil fuels emit greenhouse gases when burned, it is estimated that 60% of all manmade CO_2 in the atmosphere is from motor vehicles.

Another consequence of outdoor air pollution is acid rain. When a pollutant, such as sulfuric acid, combines with droplets of water in the air, the water (or snow) can become acidified. The effects of acid rain on the environment can be very serious. It damages plants by destroying their leaves, it poisons the soil, and it changes the chemistry of lakes and streams. Damage due to acid rain kills trees and harms animals, fish, and other wildlife. The U.S. Geological Survey (USGS), the Environmental Protection Agency (EPA), and Environment Canada are among the organizations that are actively studying the acid rain problem.

The Greenhouse Effect, also referred to as global warming, is generally believed to come from the buildup of carbon dioxide gas in the atmosphere. Carbon dioxide is produced when fuels are burned. Plants convert carbon dioxide back to oxygen, but the release of carbon dioxide from human activities is higher than the world's plants can process. The situation is made worse since many of the earth's forests are being removed, and plant life is being damaged by acid rain. Thus, the amount of carbon dioxide in the air is continuing to increase. This buildup acts like a blanket and traps heat close to the surface of our earth. Changes of even a few degrees will affect us all through changes in the climate and even the possibility that the polar ice caps may melt. One of the consequences of polar ice cap melting would be a rise in global sea level, resulting in widespread coastal flooding.

Ozone depletion is another result of pollution. Chemicals released by our activities affect the stratosphere, one of the atmospheric layers surrounding earth. The ozone layer in the stratosphere protects the earth from harmful ultraviolet radiation from the sun. Release of chlorofluorocarbons (CFC's) from aerosol cans, cooling systems and refrigerator equipment removes some of the ozone, causing "holes"; to open up in this layer and allowing the radiation to reach the earth. Ultraviolet radiation is known to cause skin cancer and has damaging effects on plants and wildlife.

Air pollution can affect our health in many ways with both short-term and long-term effects. Different groups of individuals are affected by air pollution in different ways. Some individuals are much more sensitive to pollutants than are others. Young children and elderly people often suffer more from the effects of air pollution. People with health problems such as asthma, heart and lung disease may also suffer more when the air is polluted. The extent to which an individual is harmed by air pollution usually depends on the total exposure to the damaging chemicals, i.e., the duration of exposure and the concentration of the chemicals must be taken into account.

Examples of short-term effects include irritation to the eyes, nose and throat, and upper respiratory infections such as bronchitis and pneumonia. Other symptoms can include headaches, nausea, and allergic reactions. Short-term air pollution can aggravate the medical conditions of individuals with asthma and emphysema. In the great "Smog Disaster" in London in 1952, four thousand people died in a few days due to the high concentrations of pollution.

Long-term health effects can include chronic respiratory disease, lung cancer, heart disease, and even damage to the brain, nerves, liver, or kidneys. Continual exposure to air pollution affects the lungs of growing children and may aggravate or complicate medical conditions in the elderly. It is estimated that half a million people die prematurely every year in the United States as a result of smoking cigarettes.

Research into the health effects of air pollution is ongoing. Medical conditions arising from air pollution can be very expensive. Healthcare costs, lost productivity in the workplace, and human welfare impacts cost billions of dollars each year.

In many countries in the world, steps are being taken to stop the damage to our environment from air pollution. Scientific groups study the damaging effects on plant, animal and human life. Legislative bodies write laws to control emissions. Educators in schools and universities teach students, beginning at very young ages, about the effects of air pollution.

The first step to solving air pollution is assessment. Researchers have investigated outdoor air pollution and have developed standards for measuring the type and amount of some serious air pollutants.

Scientists must then determine how much exposure to pollutants is harmful.

Once exposure levels have been set, steps can be undertaken to reduce exposure to air pollution. These can be accomplished by regulation of man-made pollution through legislation. Many countries have set controls on pollution emissions for transportation vehicles and industry. This is usually done through a variety of coordinating agencies that monitor the air and the environment. At the United Nations, the Atmosphere Management Program carries out world-wide environmental projects. In the United States, the primary federal agency is the Environmental Protection Agency. Many state and local organizations also participate in monitoring and controlling the environment.

Prevention is another key to controlling air pollution. The regulatory agencies mentioned above play an essential role in reducing and preventing air pollution in the environment.

In addition, it is possible to prevent many types of air pollution that are not regulated through personal, careful attention to our interactions with the environment. In the United States, most household products come with instructions about safe use. Building materials should be reviewed for potential harmful effects.

Northeastern America has the worst air quality in the country. This is caused in large part because it is the most densely populated section of the country. Where people are pollution seems to inevitably follow. More people results in more pollution from cars, more pollution from people smoking, and more industry. Northeastern America is a highly industrialized section of the nation, and factories have a high negative impact on the air quality.

Adequate ventilation is also a key to controlling exposure to indoor air pollution. Home and work environments should be monitored for adequate air flow and have proper exhaust systems installed.

One of the most dangerous air pollutants is cigarette smoke. Restricting smoking is an important key to a healthier environment. Legislation to control smoking is in effect in some locations, but personal exposure should be monitored and limited wherever possible.

Only through the efforts of scientists, business leaders, legislators, and individuals can we reduce the amount of air pollution on the planet. This challenge must be met by all of us in order to assure that a healthy environment will exist for ourselves and our children.

Black carbon pollution is the release of tiny particles into the air from burning fuel for energy. Air pollution caused by such particulates has been a major problem since the beginning of the industrial revolution and the development of the internal combustion engine. Scientific publications dealing with the analysis of soot and smoke date back as early as 1896. Mankind has become so dependent on the burning of fossil fuels (petroleum products, coal, and natural gas) that the sum total of all combustion-related emissions now constitutes a serious and widespread problem, not only to human health, but also to the entire global environment.

Fossil fuels account for about 88% of energy consumption in the United States. Of that, around 40% is oil, 20% is natural gas, and 20% is coal. Many people just think of oil as the stuff that makes cars run, but it is also used in diesel fuel, wax, paraffin wax, motor oil, plastic, tar, asphalt, and other products. At this point in time, dependence is so great on fossil fuels that it would be nearly impossible to live life in a civilized society without it.

Planting Trees

The Queensland government supported Greenfleet in planting two million trees in Australia between 1997 and 2005. The trees will not only soak up CO_2 emitted from cars, but will also restore habitats and reduce soil erosion. Greenfleet continues to plant trees, protecting some of Australia's threatened animals such as the false water rat, and the square tailed kite.

DRINKING WATER QUALITY AND SUPPLY

The United States has one of the safest water supplies in the world. However, national statistics don't tell you specifically about the quality and safety of the water coming out of your tap. That's because drinking water quality varies from place to place, depending on the condition of the source water from which it is drawn and the treatment it receives.

Now you have a new way to find information about your drinking water, if it comes from a public water supplier. The EPA doesn't regulate private wells, but does have recommendations for their owners. Every community water supplier must provide an annual report (sometimes called a consumer confidence report) to its customers. The report provides information on your local drinking water quality, including the water's source, the contaminants found in the water, and how consumers can get involved in protecting drinking water.

People who travel abroad know the familiar problem with unsafe drinking water. At home, we scarcely give it a thought. Usually, we are right. But the sources of our drinking water are constantly under siege from naturally occurring events and human activities that can pollute our sources of drinking water.

The Ogallala Aquifer, or the High Plains Aquifer, is a water table located beneath the Great Plains region of the United States. The Ogallala Aquifer is vast and includes the states of South Dakota, Nebraska, Wyoming, Colorado, Kansas, Oklahoma, New Mexico, and Texas. The Ogallala Aquifer is a well used source of water in the area. It provides much of the household water and a large portion of the irrigation water.

Because of the extensive use, the Ogallala Aquifer is becoming both depleted and polluted. Not only is the water supply the basis of the economy in the area, but depletion also becomes a problem when it causes large sinkholes in the land above. It is thought that 3.5 million acres of the area may be converted to dry land farming because of the depletion. For this reason management of the supply has become an important issue.

Environmental Science

DID YOU KNOW?

In the United States, water utilities treat nearly 34 billion gallons of water every day. In the United States and Canada, the total miles of water pipeline and aqueducts equal approximately one million miles; enough to circle the globe 40 times. Americans drink more than one billion glasses of tap water per day.

Children in the first six months of life consume seven times as much water per pound as the average American adult.

Safe drinking water depends on all of us doing our part in getting to know about it and protecting it.

BE INFORMED!

Read the annual Consumer Confidence Report provided by your public water system, sometimes referred to as a Water Quality Report.

If you are one of the 15 percent of Americans who have their own sources of drinking water, such as wells, cisterns, and springs, you are responsible for protecting your water supply. Find out what activities are taking place in your watershed that may impact your drinking water; talk with local experts, test your water periodically, maintain your well, close it properly.

DON'T CONTAMINATE!

- Reduce paved areas. Use permeable surfaces that allow rain to soak in, not run off, like wood, brick and gravel for decks, patios and walkways.
- Reduce or eliminate pesticide application.
- Test your soil before applying chemicals, and design your lawn and garden with hardy plants that require little or no watering, fertilizers or pesticides.
- Reduce the amount of trash you create. Reuse containers, recycle plastics, aluminum, and glass.
- Recycle used oil. A single quart of motor oil can contaminate up to 2 million gallons of drinking water; take used oil or antifreeze to a service station or recycling center.
- Take the bus instead of your car one day a week. On average, you will prevent 33 pounds of carbon dioxide emissions per day. Be careful what you put into your septic system: Harmful chemicals may end up in your drinking water.
- Keep pollutants away from boat marinas and the waterways. Keep boat motors well-tuned to prevent fuel and lubricant leaks; select nontoxic cleaning products and use a drop cloth, and clean and maintain boats away from the water.

WASTEWATER TREATMENT

We consider wastewater treatment as water use because it is so interconnected with the other uses of water. Much of the water used by homes, industries, and businesses must be treated before it is released back to the environment.

If the term "wastewater treatment" is confusing to you, then think of it as "sewage treatment." Nature has an amazing ability to cope with small amounts of water wastes and pollution, but it would be overwhelmed if we didn't treat the billions of gallons of wastewater and sewage produced every day before releasing it back to the environment. Treatment plants reduce pollutants in wastewater to a level nature can handle.

Wastewater is used water. It includes substances such as human waste, food scraps, oils, soaps and chemicals. In homes, this includes water from sinks, showers, bathtubs, toilets, washing machines and dishwashers. Businesses and industries also contribute their share of used water that must be cleaned.

Wastewater also includes storm runoff. Although some people assume that the rain that runs down the street during a storm is fairly clean, it isn't. Harmful substances that wash off roads, parking lots, and rooftops can harm our rivers and lakes.

WHY TREAT WASTEWATER?

It's a matter of caring for our environment and for our own health. There are many good reasons why keeping our water clean is an important priority:

- Fisheries - Clean water is critical to plants and animals that live in water. This is important to the fishing industry, sport fishing enthusiasts, and future generations.
- Wildlife Habitats - Our rivers and ocean waters teem with life that depends on shoreline, beaches and marshes. They are critical habitats for hundreds of species of fish and other aquatic life. Migratory water birds use the areas for resting and feeding.
- Recreation and Quality of Life - Water is a great playground for us all. The scenic and recreational values of our waters are reasons many people choose to live where they do. Visitors are drawn to water activities such as swimming, fishing, boating and picnicking.
- Health Concerns - If it is not properly cleaned, water can carry disease. Since we live, work and play so close to water, harmful bacteria have to be removed to make water safe.

The major aim of wastewater treatment is to remove as much of the suspended solids as possible before the remaining water, called effluent, is discharged back to the environment. As solid material decays, it uses up oxygen, which is needed by the plants and animals living in the water.

"Primary treatment" removes about 60 percent of suspended solids from wastewater. This treatment also involves aerating (stirring up) the wastewater, to put oxygen back in. Secondary treatment removes more than 90 percent of suspended solids.

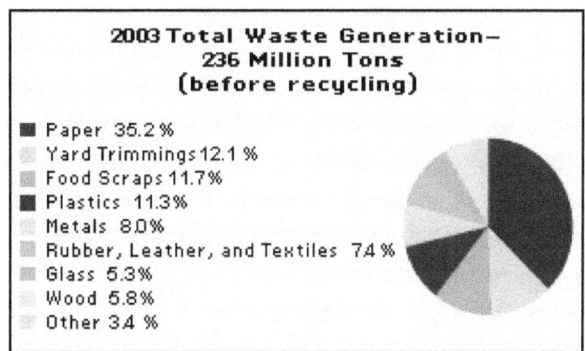

Wastewater, or sewage, must undergo a few different treatment steps, which are designed to remove different types of pollutants. The first step is called the preliminary treatment. In this step debris, such as plastic bags, are removed. This is done by filtering the water through a bar screen. This is a screen which consists of a row of bars which large debris gets collected behind, while the rest of the sewage can still flow through.

The water is then moved into a tank, and sand and dirt particles are allowed to settle so they can be removed. The second step is called primary treatment. This step consists of the removal of particulate organic material. This includes food and fecal matter particles. The particulate material settles at the bottom to be removed, and the oily material to float to the top to be removed.

The third step is called secondary treatment. In this step, dissolved organic material is removed. This is done using bacteria and other detritus feeders. The final step is called advanced treatment and consists of the removal of dissolved inorganic material. In order for a treatment to be considered a complete treatment, it must contain all four steps.

The final step of wastewater treatment consists of removing dissolved inorganic material. This refers to nutrients such as phosphorus and nitrogen. Nitrogen is removed through the process of nitrification followed by denitrification. In nitrification, ammonia is converted into nitrates. In denitrification, nitrates combine to form nitrogen gas. Phosphorus is removed through the use of bacteria. Bacteria absorbs the phosphorus, and are then removed.

MUNICIPAL SOLID WASTE (MSW)

MSW—more commonly known as trash or garbage—consists of everyday items such as product packaging, grass clippings, furniture, clothing, bottles, food scraps, newspapers, appliances, paint, and batteries.

In 2003, U.S. residents, businesses, and institutions produced more than 236 million tons of MSW, which is approximately 4.5 pounds of waste per person per day.

Several MSW management practices, such as source reduction, recycling, and composting, prevent or divert materials from the wastestream. Source reduction involves altering the design, manufacture, or use of products and materials to reduce the amount and toxicity of what gets thrown away. Recycling diverts items, such as paper, glass, plastic, and metals, from the wastestream. These materials are sorted, collected, and processed and then manufactured, sold, and bought as new products. Composting decomposes organic waste, such as food scraps and yard trimmings, with microorganisms (mainly bacteria and fungi), producing a humus-like substance.

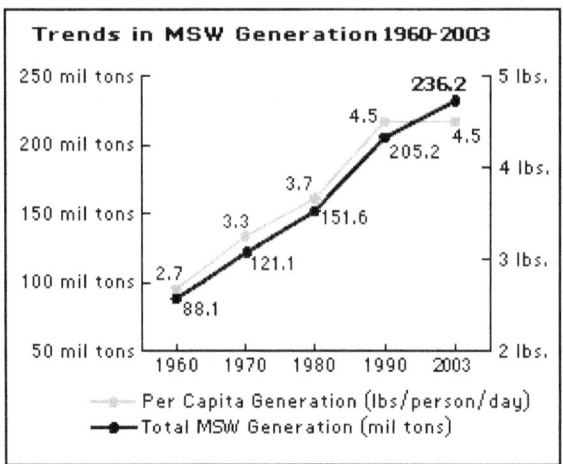

Other practices address those materials that require disposal. Landfills are engineered areas where waste is placed into the land. Landfills usually have liner systems and other safeguards to prevent groundwater contamination. Combustion is another MSW practice that has helped reduce the amount of landfill space needed. Combustion facilities burn MSW at a high temperature, reducing waste volume and generating electricity.

The United States is the largest producer of waste in the world. It is estimated that 236 million tons of waste are produced annually. While only five percent of the world's population resides in the United States, it consumes 30% of the world's resources and produces 30% of the world's trash.

SOLID WASTE HIERARCHY

The EPA has ranked the most environmentally sound strategies for MSW. Source reduction (including reuse) is the most preferred method, followed by recycling and composting, and, lastly, disposal in combustion facilities and landfills. Currently, in the United States, 30 percent is recovered and recycled or composted, 14 percent is burned at combustion facilities, and the remaining 56 percent is disposed of in landfills.

LANDFILLS

Today's landfills are very different from the open dumps of the past. For one thing, new landfills are situated where clay deposits and other land features act as natural buffers between the landfills and the surrounding environment.

Second, the bottom and sides of modern landfills are lined with layers of clay or plastic to keep the liquid waste, called leachate, from escaping into the soil.

A network of drains collects the leachate and pumps it to the surface where it can be treated. Ground wells are also drilled into and around the landfill to monitor groundwater quality and to detect any contamination. These safety measures keep ground water, which is the main source of drinking water in many communities, clean and pure.

To protect the environment even more, the landfill is divided into a series of individual cells. Only a few cells of the site (called the working face) are filled with trash at any one time, minimizing exposure to wind and rain.

At the end of each day's activities, workers spread a layer of earth—called the daily cover—over the waste to reduce odor and control vermin. The workers fill and cap each cell with a layer of clay and earth, and then seed the area with native grasses.

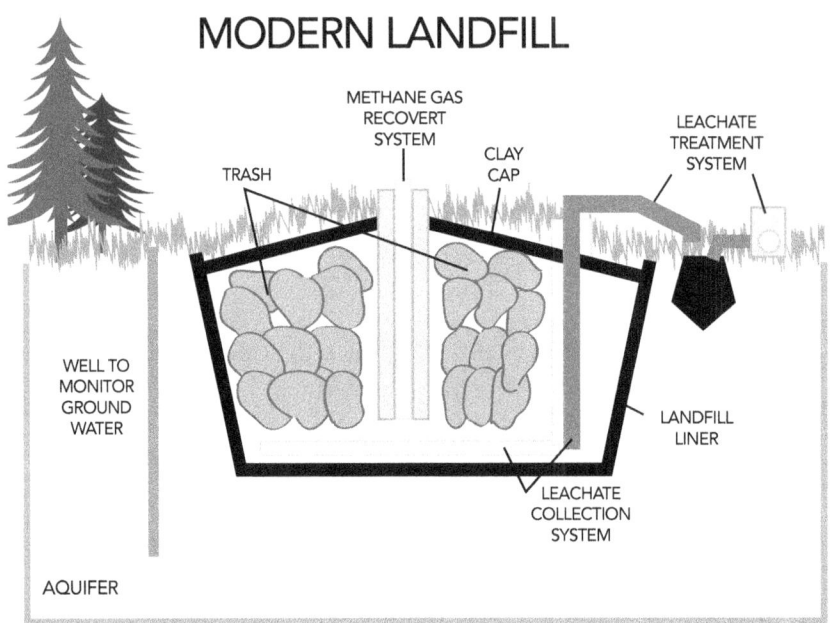

When a landfill is full, workers seal and cover the landfill with a final cap of clay and dirt. Workers continue to monitor the ground wells for years after a landfill is closed to keep tabs on the quality of groundwater on and around the site.

Old landfill sites can be landscaped to blend in with their surroundings, or specially developed to provide an asset to a community. Closed landfills can be turned into anything from parks to parking lots, from golf courses to ski slopes. Building homes and businesses on these sites is generally not permitted, though, since it can take many years for the ground to settle.

Biodegradation is a natural process. It happens when microorganisms, such as fungi or bacteria, secrete enzymes that chemically break down or degrade dead plants and animals. In other words, biodegradation is when waste decays or rots. Most organic wastes are biodegradable under normal environmental conditions. Given enough time, the waste will disintegrate into harmless substances, enriching the soil with nutrients.

A landfill is not a normal environmental condition, though, nor is it intended to be. Instead, a landfill is more like a tightly sealed storage container. A landfill is designed to inhibit degradation to protect the environment from harmful contamination. Deprived of air and water, even organic wastes—like paper and grass clippings—degrade very slowly in a landfill.

Landfills are a common way of disposing trash. The theory of a landfill is to contain wastes in drums and then bury them in the ground. The wells in the area are monitored to ensure that the landfills are properly containing any possibly hazardous materials.

A study by the Environmental Protection Agency (EPA) showed that 40% of all waste in landfills was actually paper. This is a disturbing thought because essentially all paper products are recyclable, meaning that it isn't necessary to dump them in landfills where the space is much better used on other products.

BIOREACTOR LANDFILLS

A new approach to landfills is designing them so that organic waste is allowed to biodegrade. These landfills, called bioreactors, are different than most landfills used today.

One type of bioreactor is aerobic (with air). Leachate is removed from the bottom layer of the landfill and put into storage tanks. The leachate is then pumped back into the landfill, allowing it to flow over the waste repeatedly. Air is then added to the landfill. This type of bioreactor models normal air and moisture environmental conditions better than other landfills and encourages the natural process of biodegrading.

Another type of bioreactor is anaerobic (without air). In this type of landfill, air is not added, but the leachate is collected and pumped back into the landfill. Additional liquids may also be added to the leachate to help the waste biodegrade. Because the waste is broken down without oxygen, anaerobic bioreactors produce landfill gas, or methane, which can be used as an energy source.

Bioreactor landfills have advantages over traditional landfills. They reduce the cost of removing and disposing of leachated, which is used on site. Anaerobic bioreactors begin producing methane much more quickly than landfills designed to inhibit degradation. bioreactors also gain space as the waste degrades, meaning more waste can be added.

LANDFILL ENERGY

Landfills can be sources of energy. Organic waste produces a gas called methane as it decomposes, or rots. Methane is the same energy-rich gas that is in natural gas, the fuel sold by natural gas utility companies. Methane gas is colorless and odorless. Natural gas utilities add an odorant so people can detect seeping gas, but it can be dangerous to people or the environment. New rules require landfills to collect methane gas as a pollution and safety measure.

Some landfills simply burn the methane gas in a controlled fashion to get rid of it. But the methane can be used as an energy source. Landfills can collect the methane gas, treat it, and then sell it as a commercial fuel; or they can burn it to generate steam and electricity. In 2003, East Kentucky Power Cooperative began recovering methane gas from three landfills. The utility uses the landfill gas to generate 8.8 megawatts of electricity, enough power 7,500-8,000 homes.

Today, there are almost 400 operating landfill gas energy projects in the United States. California has the most projects in operation with 73, followed by Illinois with 36 and Michigan with 27. The United States Environmental Protection Agency examined landfill conditions throughout the nation and almost every state has at least one landfill that would likely produce methane gas for energy use.

SOURCE REDUCTION (WASTE PREVENTION)

Source reduction can be a successful method of reducing waste generation. Practices such as grasscycling, backyard composting, two-sided copying of paper, and transport packaging reduction by industry have yielded substantial benefits through source reduction.

Source reduction has many environmental benefits. It prevents emissions of many greenhouse gases, reduces pollutants, saves energy, conserves resources, and reduces the need for new landfills and combustors.

RECYCLING

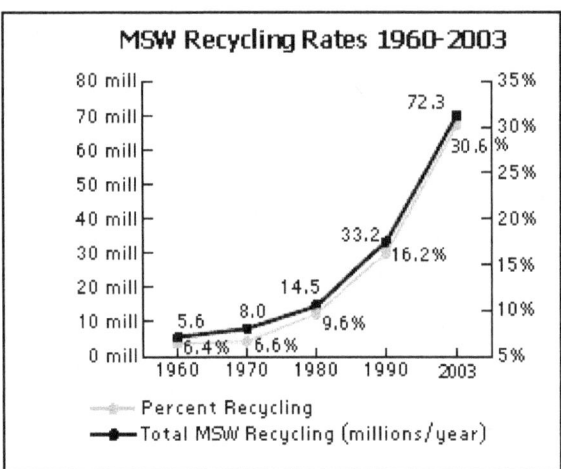

Recycling, including composting, diverted 72 million tons of material away from disposal in 2003, up from 15 million tons in 1980, when the recycle rate was just 10% and 90% of MSW was being recycled.

Typical materials that are recycled include batteries, recycled at a rate of 93%, paper and paperboard at 48%, and yard trimmings at 56%. These materials and others may be recycled through curbside programs, drop-off centers, buy-back programs, and deposit systems.

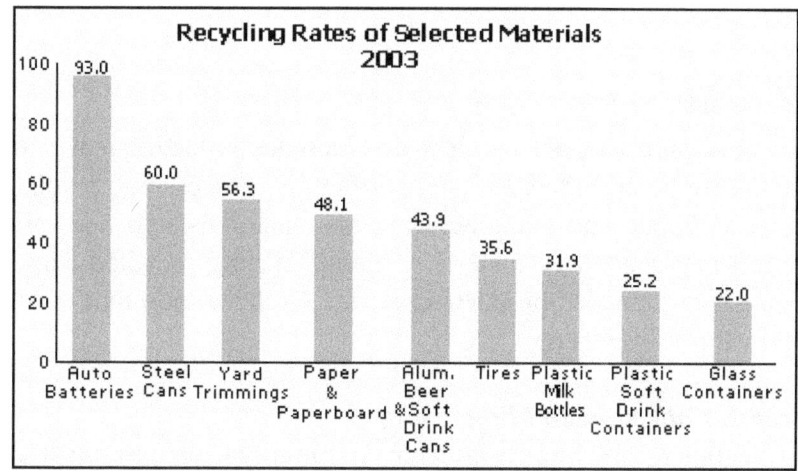

Recycling prevents the emission of many greenhouse gases and water pollutants, saves energy, supplies valuable raw materials to industry, creates jobs, stimulates the development of greener technologies, conserves resources for our children's future, and reduces the need for new landfills and combustors.

Recycling also helps reduce greenhouse gas emissions that affect global climate. In 1996, recycling of solid waste in the United States prevented the release of 33 million tons of carbon into the air—roughly the amount emitted annually by 25 million cars.

COMBUSTION/INCINERATION

Burning MSW can generate energy while reducing the amount of waste by up to 90 percent in volume and 75 percent in weight.

The EPA's Office of Air and Radiation is primarily responsible for regulating combustors because air emissions from combustion pose the greatest environmental concern. In 2001, in the United States, there were 97 combustors with energy recovery with the capacity to burn up to 95,000 tons of MSW per day.

LANDFILLS

Under the Resource Conservation and Recovery Act (RCRA), landfills that accept MSW are primarily regulated by state, tribal, and local governments. The EPA, however, has established national standards these landfills must meet in order to stay open. Municipal landfills can, however, accept household hazardous waste.

The number of landfills in the United States is steadily decreasing—from 8,000 in 1988 to 1,767 in 2002. The capacity, however, has remained relatively constant. New landfills are much larger than in the past.

RECYCLING

Recycling is a series of activities that includes collecting recyclable materials that would otherwise be considered waste, sorting and processing recyclables into raw materials such as fibers, and manufacturing raw materials into new products. Collecting and processing secondary materials, manufacturing recycled-content products, and then purchasing recycled products creates a circle or loop that ensures the overall success and value of recycling.

Step 1. Collection and Processing
Collecting recyclables varies from community to community, but there are four primary methods: curbside, drop-off centers, buy-back centers, and deposit/refund programs.

Regardless of the method used to collect the recyclables, the next leg of their journey is usually the same. Recyclables are sent to a materials recovery facility to be sorted and prepared into marketable commodities for manufacturing. Recyclables are bought and sold just like any other commodity, and prices for the materials change and fluctuate with the market.

Step 2. Manufacturing
Once cleaned and separated, the recyclables are ready to undergo the second part of the recycling loop. More and more of today's products are being manufactured with total or partial recycled content. Common household items that contain recycled materials include newspapers and paper towels; aluminum, plastic, and glass soft drink containers; steel cans; and plastic laundry detergent bottles. Recycled materials also are used in innovative applications such as recovered glass in roadway asphalt (glassphalt) or recovered plastic in carpeting, park benches, and pedestrian bridges.

Step 3. Purchasing Recycled Products
Purchasing recycled products completes the recycling loop. By "buying recycled," governments, as well as businesses and individual consumers, each play an important role in making the recycling process a success. As consumers demand more environmentally sound products, manufacturers will continue to meet that demand by producing high-quality recycled products.

RECYCLING FACTS AND FIGURES

- In 1999, recycling and composting activities prevented about 64 million tons of material from ending up in landfills and incinerators. Today, this country recycles 28 percent of its waste, a rate that has almost doubled during the past 15 years.

- While recycling has grown in general, recycling of specific materials has grown even more drastically: 42 percent of all paper, 40 percent of all plastic soft drink bottles, 55 percent of all aluminum beer and soft drink cans, 57 percent of all steel packaging, and 52 percent of all major appliances are now recycled.

- Twenty years ago, only one curbside recycling program existed in the United States, which collected several materials at the curb. By 1998, 9,000 curbside programs and 12,000 recyclable drop-off centers had sprouted up across the nation. As of 1999, 480 materials recovery facilities have been established to process the collected materials.

MASS TRANSIT

Mass transit, or public transportation, refers to transportation systems which are available to the general public. This can include busses, trams, subways and other such transportation systems. However, transportation methods such as carpooling and taxis do not fit into this category because they are considered to be a private agreement, as opposed to being open to the general public. Mass transit has shown to be much better for the environment than private transportation methods. Mass transit methods use less fuel, and emit less carbon dioxide and carbon monoxide per person than do private transportation methods.

Political Processes and the Future

ENVIRONMENTAL LAWS, POLICIES AND ETHICS

The Environmental Protection Agency, as mentioned many times in this study guide, has created many laws, policies and procedures. The efforts have resulted in many positive changes for the environment, but more importantly, for the quality of life for human beings. Some of the agency's most notable actions have been:

- Clean Air Act enacted in 1970 to regulate air pollution.
- Clean Water Act enacted in 1972 to regulate water pollution.
- Resource Conservation and Recovery Act of 1976 (RCRA), the "cradle-to-the-grave" tracking of hazardous waste.

- Toxic Substances Control Act of 1979, which requires new chemicals to be tested for carcinogenic (cancer causing) properties.

Many companies and private individuals today make decisions that impact the environment. A recent EPA campaign was focused on Fortune 500 companies making a plan and a resolve to reduce over 15 billion pounds of greenhouse gas emissions. Each company that participated not only gets publicity from the participation but nets positive results that everyone in the world will enjoy.

HOW A BILL BECOMES A LAW

Bills are proposed by members of Congress. If a bill is proposed in either the Senate or the House of Representatives, it is approved by a committee, and then recommended to the body as a whole. Then the bill can be debated, and amended, before it is read for a second time and a vote is taken. If a bill passes it is sent to the other house of Congress where the process is repeated. If it passes again it is sent to the President, who can either sign it, making it law, or veto it, in which case it is sent back to Congress for further amendments. If the President does nothing for 10 days, the bill automatically becomes law.

DIFFERING CULTURAL AND SOCIETAL VALUES

There are many different types of people in the world, all entitled to their own opinion. Each person every day makes decisions that affect the environment. Many environmentalists become frustrated in their debates because of the gap between environmental education and people's actions.

Along these lines, people in "enlightened" countries can't agree on land usage, chemical disposal, etc. As we discussed earlier, the earth has a limited amount of resources. Many groups such as the people at http://www.overpopulation.org/ are very concerned. It will be worth your time to read at least a little on their site to see how impassioned they are and how closely (or not) their views come to your own.

Statistical Analysis of Environment

J SHAPE GROWTH CURVE

The J shape curve is a way to show the population density of an organism in a new environment. The population density grows quickly until it reaches some resistance, such as a winter season or another environmental factor that limits or terminates the growth. The more organisms in a population the faster they will breed. For example,

Darwin hypothesized that one pair of elephants could product 19 million elephants over 700 years. Below is an example of the graph. The curve will become steeper with time.

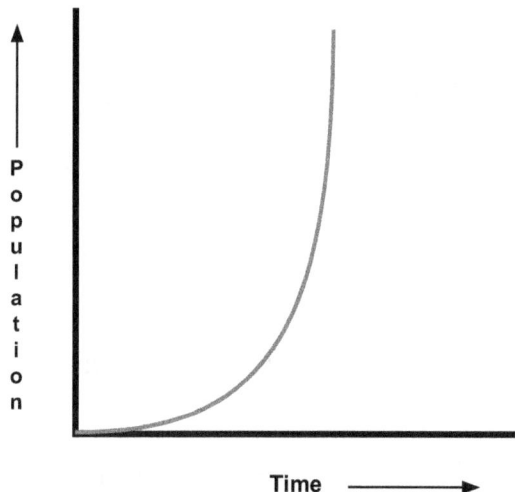

S SHAPE GROWTH CURVE

The following is an S-curve. S-curve is a shortened version of Sigmoid population curve. This diagram is used to show carrying capacity of an area. Once the organisms have reproduced, they can only continue to grow as the environment has the ability to support them. Once these resources are used up, the environment is at the carrying capacity for that organism and growth tapers off. K on the graph refers to the carrying capacity.

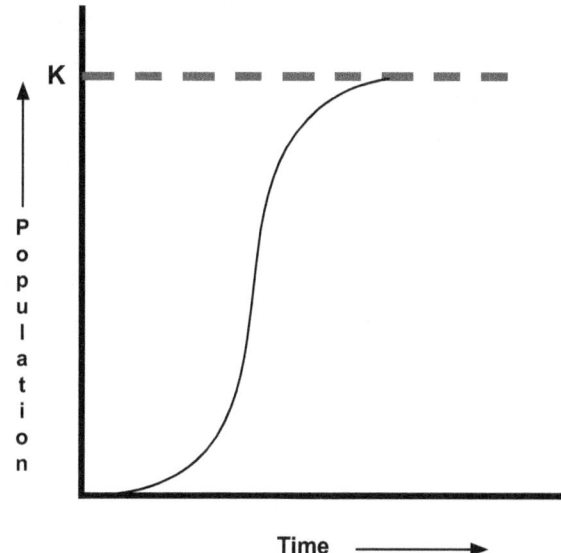

Sample Test Questions

1) Which of the following eats only meat?

    A) Omnivore
    B) Carnivore
    C) Herbivore
    D) None of the above

The correct answer is B:) Carnivore. A carnivore is a person or animal that only eats meat.

2) _____ is a group of specific species of plants, animals and microbes that interact with each other.

    A) Taiga
    B) Ecosystem
    C) Forest
    D) None of the above

The correct answer is B:) Ecosystem. An ecosystem is a group of plants, animals and microbes that interact with each other.

3) Which of the following is NOT a main category of organisms?

    A) Producers
    B) Consumers
    C) Food web
    D) Decomposers

The correct answer is C:) Food web. The food web shows how different organisms, producers, consumers and decomposers interact with each other.

4) In which layer of the atmosphere is it bad to have O3 in?

   A) Chemosphere
   B) Mesosphere
   C) Stratosphere
   D) Troposphere

The correct answer is D:) Troposphere. Because there is a lot of vertical movement within the troposphere it would be dangerous to have ozone in it because ozone absorbs radiation.

5) Which of the following describes biomagnification?

   A) Looking at a living object under a microscope to make it easier to see.
   B) The process by which the concentration of a specific species increases in a given environment.
   C) When the concentration of a substance increases as it moves through the food chain.
   D) Another name for bioaccumulation.

The correct answer is C:) When the concentration of a substance increases as it moves through the food chain. Answer D is not correct because biomagnification is a result of bioaccumulation, not another name for it.

6) Which of the following is an inorganic substance?

   A) Plants
   B) Raccoon
   C) Rocks
   D) Worms

The correct answer is C:) Rocks. Rocks are not alive so they are not organic.

7) A dark brown spongy residue from organic materials

   A) Loam
   B) Humus
   C) Lipids
   D) Sludge cake

The correct answer is B:) Humus. Humus is a dark spongy residue from organic materials.

8) What are pond pioneers?

   A) Algae and other submerged plants which develop in the beginning stages of pond succession.
   B) The animals which begin to inhabit a pond as pond succession proceeds.
   C) Plants which cover the surface of a pond as it begins to fill in.
   D) None of the above

The correct answer is A:) Algae and other submerged plants which develop in the beginning stages of pond succession.

9) Water covers what percentage of the earth?

   A) 25%
   B) 50%
   C) 75%
   D) 85%

The correct answer is C:) 75%. Water covers approximately 75% of the earth.

10) Which of the following is NOT organic?

   A) Water
   B) Insects
   C) Bears
   D) Humans

The correct answer is A:) Water. Water is not organic.

11) What is the difference between biomagnification and bioaccumulation?

   A) Biomagnification is when toxins build up in an organism, and bioaccumulation is what occurs when the organism is consumed by another.
   B) Because of biomagnification, bioaccumulation occurs when an organism is consumed.
   C) Because of bioaccumulation, biomagnification occurs when an organism is consumed.
   D) There is no difference. The two terms describe the same process.

The correct answer is C:) Because of bioaccumulation, biomagnification occurs when an organism is consumed. Biomagnification is a compounding of the concentrations of a toxin which occurs through consuming an organism in which bioaccumulation has occurred.

12) _____ is what all living things are composed of.

   A) Water
   B) Nitrate
   C) Carbon
   D) Methane

The correct answer is C:) Carbon. All living things are composed of carbon.

13) Energy from all food begins where?

   A) At the producer
   B) At the sun
   C) At the soil
   D) In the animal consuming it

The correct answer is B:) At the sun. Energy from all food begins at the sun. Grasses (producers) need sun to grow. When something consumes that producer, it is consuming the energy that originally came from the sun.

14) What is meant by the phrase sustainable living?

   A) Eating healthy food to sustain your energy throughout the day.
   B) Living in a way that can be continued as time progresses.
   C) Continuing life in the same way, without regard for the world's resources.
   D) All of the above describe sustainable living.

The correct answer is B:) Living in a way that can be continued as time progresses. This idea developed because resources are not infinite, and the current method of life for many people cannot be indefinitely sustained.

15) These types of organisms get their energy from consuming other organisms

   A) Producer
   B) Primary producer
   C) Consumer
   D) Omnivore

The correct answer is C:) Consumer. Consumers get their energy from eating other consumers or producers.

16) _____ is calculated by the number of live births per 1000 population.

    A) Birth rate
    B) Death rate
    C) Infant mortality rate
    D) Fetal death rate

The correct answer is A:) Birth rate. Birth rate is calculated by the number of live births per 1000 population.

17) Death rate is calculated by the number of deaths in a year per _____ population.

    A) 100
    B) 1000
    C) 10,000
    D) 100,000

The correct answer is D:) 100,000. Death rate is calculated by the number of deaths in a year per 100,000 population.

18) What is the term for the process whereby substances build up in the body?

    A) Bioaccumulation
    B) Biomagnification
    C) Eutrophication
    D) Biochemication

The correct answer is A:) Bioaccumulation. When substances accumulate, or build up, in the body it is called bioaccumulation.

19) Which of the following are NOT principles of ecosystem sustainability?

    A) Disposes of wastes and replenishes nutrients
    B) Use sunlight as their only source of energy
    C) Consumer populations are unrestricted
    D) Biodiversity is maintained

The correct answer is C:) Consumer populations are unrestricted. Ecosystem sustainability relies on answers A and D to maintain balance.

20) What is a steppe?

   A) A large flat area of land which is generally covered with short grasses.
   B) A specific type of veldt found in southern Africa.
   C) A breed of animal which is found only in the plains of southern Africa.
   D) None of the above

The correct answer is A:) A large flat area of land which is generally covered with short grasses. Steppes are generally used for grazing livestock or growing wheat.

21) Acid rain does NOT fall to the earth in what form?

   A) Fog
   B) Rain
   C) Snow
   D) None of the above

The correct answer is D:) None of the above. Acid rain can occur in fog, rain and snow.

22) Barren rocks would be the location of

   A) Primary succession
   B) Secondary succession
   C) Tertiary succession
   D) None of the above

The correct answer is A:) Primary succession. Succession is when a plant or organism takes over a new area. It is the primary succession because it occurs in an area devoid of life, such as rocks or lava.

23) Which of the following could describe cultural eutrophication?

   A) When an excess of algae growth occurs naturally, and foul smelling waste accumulates.
   B) When pollution causes an excess of algae growth, eventually leading to the accumulation of foul smelling waste.
   C) Both of the above
   D) None of the above

The correct answer is B:) When pollution causes an excess of algae growth, eventually leading to the accumulation of foul smelling waste. Answer A could not be correct because it describes natural eutrophication, not cultural eutrophication.

24) _____ is when so many nutrients are brought to a body of water that algae grows abundantly, consuming all the oxygen in the water.

    A) Eutrophication
    B) Turbid
    C) Desertification
    D) Deforestation

The correct answer is A:) Eutrophication. Eutrophication is when so many nutrients are brought to a body of water that algae grows abundantly, consuming all the oxygen in the water.

25) The One Birth Policy is a law in which country?

    A) Russia
    B) Denmark
    C) India
    D) China

The correct answer is D:) China. This policy was instituted in order to control the population growth.

26) Which of the following eats both meat and plants?

    A) Omnivore
    B) Carnivore
    C) Herbivore
    D) None of the above

The correct answer is A:) Omnivore. An omnivore eats both plants and animals (or meat).

27) Which of the following is NOT a problem related to the Ogallala Aquifer.

    A) Depletion
    B) Sinkholes
    C) Pollution
    D) Flooding

The correct answer is D:) Flooding. The Ogallala Aquifer is becoming depleted. Flooding is the opposite of the problem.

28) Which countries have the least and most energy used per person respectively?

   A) Denmark, China
   B) India, USA
   C) Bangladesh, USA
   D) China, Russia

The correct answer is C:) Bangladesh, USA.

29) When water is nutrient rich it is called

   A) Oligotrophic
   B) Turbid
   C) Murky
   D) Eutrophic

The correct answer is D:) Eutrophic. Another name for nutrient rich water is eutrophic.

30) Which of the following carry sediment?

   A) Lakes
   B) Rivers
   C) Dams
   D) Reservoirs

The correct answer is B:) Rivers. Rivers carry sediment along their course.

31) Which of the following is a benefit of planting trees?

   A) Absorb CO2 from the air
   B) Reduced soil erosion
   C) Protect threatened animals
   D) All of the above

The correct answer is D:) All of the above. Answers A, B and C all state benefits of planting trees.

32) An abandoned farm field would be the location of

   A) Primary succession
   B) Secondary succession
   C) Tertiary succession
   D) None of the above

The correct answer is B:) Secondary succession. Succession is when a plant or organism takes over a new area. It is the secondary succession because it occurs in an area that already has life.

33) What is it called when a lake bottom is gradually built up over years?

   A) Aquatic succession
   B) Saltwater intrusion
   C) Land subsidence
   D) Sinkhole

The correct answer is A:) Aquatic succession. Aquatic succession is when a lake bottom is gradually built up.

34) Which of the following generally indicates low energy consumption per person in a country?

   A) Small size
   B) Poor
   C) Location
   D) All of the above

The correct answer is B:) Poor. Answer choice A is incorrect because a country's size does not indicate lower energy consumption per person, just overall. However if a country is poor the people can't afford energy.

35) What is the specific name for large, open grasslands in southern Africa?

   A) Steppe
   B) Taiga
   C) Plain
   D) Veldt

The correct answer is D:) Veldt. Veldts are very similar to steppes, but the term is specific to the grasslands in southern Africa.

36) Which of the following was NOT a problem within the first human cities?

   A) Waste management
   B) Telecommunication
   C) Food scarcity
   D) Sanitation

The correct answer is B:) Telecommunication. Telecommunication was not a problem in the first human cities. They had to worry about more basic problems such as waste management and sanitation.

37) What is the difference between natural and cultural eutrophication?

   A) Natural eutrophication is a natural process occurring over thousands of years, and cultural eutrophication is the same process which has been accelerated due to the actions of humans.
   B) Natural eutrophication is a natural process occurring over thousands of years, and cultural eutrophication is the opposite process which has been accelerated due to the actions of humans.
   C) Cultural eutrophication is a natural process occurring over thousands of years, and natural eutrophication is the same process which has been accelerated due to the actions of humans.
   D) Cultural eutrophication is a natural process occurring over thousands of years, and natural eutrophication is the opposite process which has been accelerated due to the actions of humans.

The correct answer is A:) Natural eutrophication is a natural process occurring over thousands of years, and cultural eutrophication is the same process which has been accelerated due to the actions of humans.

38) What is the most used type of fossil fuel in the United States?

   A) Natural gas
   B) Crude oil
   C) Coal
   D) Nuclear power

The correct answer is B:) Crude oil.

39) The gradual increase of the earth's temperature is due to?

   A) Green Revolution
   B) Greenhouse effect
   C) Acid rain
   D) Overpopulation

The correct answer is B:) Greenhouse effect. The greenhouse effect, also known as global warming, relates to the gradual warming of the earth's temperature.

40) Which region has the worst air quality?

   A) Southwestern America
   B) Southeastern America
   C) Northeastern America
   D) Northwestern America

The correct answer is C:) Northeastern America. This is due to the high population density and high industrialization of the area.

41) Which of the following is NOT naturally occurring greenhouse gas?

   A) Carbon dioxide
   B) Methane
   C) Nitrous oxide
   D) Hydrofluorocarbons

The correct answer is D:) Hydrofluorocarbons. These are not a naturally occurring greenhouse gas.

42) The process of cutting, clearing and burning a forest

   A) Eutrophication
   B) Turbid
   C) Desertification
   D) Deforestation

The correct answer is D:) Deforestation. When a forest is cut, cleared and burned, the result is called deforestation.

43) What is the state of global population?

A) Decreasing
B) Remaining the same
C) Increasing
D) Fluctuating randomly

The correct answer is C:) Increasing. The world's population continues to grow at greater and greater intervals as time progresses.

44) Which of the following is NOT a cause of air pollution?

A) Smoking
B) Industry
C) Cars
D) All of the above cause air pollution

The correct answer is D:) All of the above cause air pollution. Answers A, B, and C are all causes of air pollution.

45) Deforestation is most likely to be done

A) In third world countries
B) In rural areas
C) In city areas
D) In developed countries

The correct answer is A:) In third world countries. Deforestation occurs mainly in third world countries because farmers are clearing the land to raise cattle or crops.

46) Which of the following is a renewable resource?

A) Coal power
B) Solar power
C) Oil
D) Electric power

The correct answer is B:) Solar power. Solar power is a renewable resource as it is constantly available and cannot be used up.

47) Through what process is nitrogen removed from wastewater?

   A) Denitrification only
   B) Nitrification only
   C) Nitrification and denitrification
   D) Bacteria absorbs all of the nitrogen

The correct answer is C:) Nitrification and denitrification. In nitrification, ammonia is converted into nitrates, and in denitrification nitrates are converted into nitrogen gas. Through this process, the nitrogen is removed from the wastewater.

48) The Green Revolution did what?

   A) Increased the amount of farm land
   B) Increased the yield on wheat crops
   C) A battle for the right to farm on your land
   D) Was a strategy to give the rights of the few to the many

The correct answer is B:) Increased the yield on wheat crops. Scientific studies and improvements resulted in a hybrid of wheat more productive to its surroundings.

49) What type of movement occurs in the troposphere and NOT the stratosphere?

   A) Vertical
   B) Paradoxical
   C) Transcal
   D) Elemental

The correct answer is A:) Vertical. This is the reason that it is dangerous to have ozone in the troposphere, but it is helpful to have it in the stratosphere.

50) Which of the following correctly describes a path through which biomagnification could occur?

   A) Fish, water, algae
   B) Water, fish, people
   C) Both of the above
   D) Neither of the above

The correct answer is B:) Water, fish, people. The answer could not be A because the substances cannot pass from the fish to the water, however B is a correct answer because the substances can pass from the water to the fish.

51) Which of the following are pests?

   A) Mice
   B) Bears
   C) Wolves
   D) Any animal destroying crops or livestock

The correct answer is D:) Any animal destroying crops or livestock. A pest is anything that interferes with the ability to raise crops. It can be an insect or animal.

52) What do detritus feeders consume?

   A) Dead plant material
   B) Live plant material
   C) Non plant material
   D) All of the above

The correct answer is A:) Dead plant material. Common detrivores include fungus, vultures, and termites.

53) Temperature increases with altitude in the

   A) Tropopause
   B) Stratosphere
   C) Troposphere
   D) Ozone shield

The correct answer is B:) Stratosphere. The stratosphere is where the temperature increases with the altitude.

54) Which of the following is NOT true of recycling?

   A) By recycling space can be saved because products are not buried in landfills or left in dumps.
   B) Recycling is essentially the process of reusing a product.
   C) Products made from metal, plastic, glass, and paper can all be recycled.
   D) All of the above are true

The correct answer is D:) All of the above are true. Answers A, B, and C are all correct statements about recycling.

55) When water becomes murky or dark it is

   A) Eutrophication
   B) Turbid
   C) Sedimentized
   D) A sink hole

The correct answer is B:) Turbid. Dark or murky water is called turbid. This dark water does not allow for light to reach plants which means there is less oxygen in the water.

56) Where do organisms in deep sea ecosystems get their energy?

   A) Gamma rays from the sun, which are invisible to the human eye, penetrate deep into the ocean giving energy to the organisms found there.
   B) Geothermally heated waters which issue from hydrothermal vents on the ocean floor.
   C) All energy is derived only through decomposing organisms which fall from the waters above.
   D) All of the above describe ways the organisms receive energy.

The correct answer is B:) Geothermally heated waters which issue from hydrothermal vents on the ocean floor. Hydrothermal vents allow organisms to thrive, where it wasn't thought life was even possible.

57) Which of the following is NOT true?

   A) If the President does not sign or veto a bill within 10 days it automatically becomes law.
   B) A bill must be proposed in the House of Representatives, never in the Senate.
   C) The President has the right to veto a law and send it back to Congress to be rewritten.
   D) All of the above are true statements

The correct answer is B:) A bill must be proposed in the House of Representatives, never in the Senate. A bill can be proposed in either house, but it must pass through both before becoming a law.

58) Biomagnification is found in what tissue?

   A) Skin
   B) Muscles
   C) Bone
   D) Fat

The correct answer is D:) Fat. Metals tend to be highly fat soluble, and therefore accumulate in fatty compounds.

59) What does an electrostatic precipitator do?

   A) Filters excess electrons from the air.
   B) Infuses the air with water droplets.
   C) Creates an electric charge in the water droplets in the air.
   D) Filters particles out of the air by creating an electric charge.

The correct answer is D:) Filters particles out of the air by creating an electric charge.

60) Which of the following must a wastewater treatment remove to be considered a complete treatment?

   A) Debris
   B) Particulate and dissolved organic material
   C) Dissolved inorganic material
   D) All of the above

The correct answer is D:) All of the above. In order for a treatment to be complete it must remove debris, such as plastic bags or sand, particulate organic material, such as food wastes, dissolved organic material, and dissolved inorganic material, such as nitrogen and phosphorus.

61) Which of the following is NOT a nonrenewable resource?

   A) Coal
   B) Oil
   C) Water
   D) Metal

The correct answer is C:) Water. Water is considered a renewable resource.

62) Chemicals that kill plants are called

   A) Pesticides
   B) Herbicides
   C) Crop dusting
   D) DDT

The correct answer is B:) Herbicides. Chemicals that kill plants are called herbicides.

63) What percentage of landfills are taken up by paper?

   A) 10%
   B) 20%
   C) 30%
   D) 40%

The correct answer is D:) 40%. Even though paper is recyclable, it is the largest component of landfills.

64) Which country produces the most waste?

   A) China
   B) Russia
   C) Mexico
   D) United States

The correct answer is D:) United States.

65) When lakes convert into forest it is called

   A) Primary succession
   B) Secondary succession
   C) Tertiary succession
   D) Aquatic succession

The correct answer is D:) Aquatic succession. Aquatic succession is when an aquatic environment changes through the force of succession.

66) Chemicals that kill insects are called

   A) Pesticides
   B) Herbicides
   C) Crop dusting
   D) Organicides

The correct answer is A:) Pesticides. Chemicals that kill insects are called pesticides.

67) This was used to control malaria in WWII

   A) Pesticides
   B) Herbicides
   C) Crop dusting
   D) DDT

The correct answer is D:) DDT. DDT is the chemical that was used in WWII to control malaria.

68) The Queensland government planted two million trees along with what other organization?

   A) Environmental Protection Agency
   B) Greenpeace
   C) Greenfleet
   D) None of the above

The correct answer is C:) Greenfleet.

69) Land subsidence is related to

   A) Sink hole
   B) Land management
   C) Wells
   D) Statuaries

The correct answer is A:) Sink hole. Land subsidence is the study of the motion of the surface of the earth. When the earth moves, sink holes can be formed.

70) Which of the following is not a part of the three Rs?

   A) Reduce
   B) Repair
   C) Re-use
   D) Recycle

The correct answer is B:) Repair. The three Rs consist of reduce, re-use, recycle.

71) Through what process is phosphorus removed from wastewater?

   A) Nitrification and denitrification
   B) Nitrification only
   C) Denitrification only
   D) Bacteria absorbs the phosphorus and are removed

The correct answer is D:) Bacteria absorbs the phosphorus and are removed. Nitrification and denitrification describe the process by which nitrogen is removed from wastewater, not phosphorus.

72) What is the preferred elimination method of waste?

   A) Dumps
   B) Recycling
   C) Landfills
   D) Burning

The correct answer is B:) Recycling. Recycling, or reusing, is the safest and most environmentally healthy way to dispose of waste.

73) What is the biggest component of landfills?

   A) Metal
   B) Glass
   C) Paper
   D) Plastic

The correct answer is C:) Paper. Although paper is recyclable, it has become the largest component of landfills.

74) The part of precipitation that does not soak into the ground

   A) Leachate
   B) Seep
   C) Runoff
   D) Reverse osmosis

The correct answer is C:) Runoff. Runoff is water that does not soak into the ground.

75) What is the process called by which a pond fills into land?

   A) Pond transformation
   B) Landification
   C) Pond succession
   D) None of the above

The correct answer is C:) Pond succession. This is a process which occurs over many hundreds of years.

76) Materials in the soil dissolving and seeping to the groundwater

   A) Runoff
   B) Seeping
   C) Reverse osmosis
   D) Leaching

The correct answer is D:) Leaching. Leaching is when chemicals in the soil seep into the groundwater.

77) What percentage of the world's trash is produced by the United States?

   A 10%
   B) 30%
   C) 50%
   D) 70%

The correct answer is B:) 30%. Although only 5% of the world's population resides in the United States, 30% of the world's trash originates there.

78) A solid which consists of a mixture of 40% sand, 40% silt and 20% clay.

    A) Loam
    B) Humus
    C) Lipids
    D) Sludge cake

The correct answer is A:) Loam. Loam is a type of dirt which consists of 40% sand, 40% silt and 20% clay.

79) The maximum population that an area can support is called

    A) Carrying capacity
    B) Birth rate
    C) Biodiversity rate
    D) Biome mass

The correct answer is A:) Carrying capacity. Carrying capacity is the maximum population that an area can support.

80) In what way do mass transit programs help the environment?

    A) Use less fuel per person
    B) Emit more carbon dioxide per person
    C) Emit more carbon monoxide per person
    D) All of the above

The correct answer is A:) Use less fuel per person. Answers B and C are incorrect because mass transit systems emit less carbon dioxide and carbon monoxide per person, not more.

81) What layer of the atmosphere does the ozone reside in?

    A) Troposphere
    B) Stratosphere
    C) Lithosphere
    D) Mesosphere

The correct answer is B:) Stratosphere. Because the stratosphere contains ozone, the temperature actually increases because of the radiation absorption.

82) The area of the atmosphere where temperatures are reversed

   A) Tropopause
   B) Stratosphere
   C) Troposphere
   D) Ozone shield

The correct answer is A:) Tropopause. Tropopause is the area of the atmosphere where temperatures are reversed.

83) Which of the following are NOT producers?

   A) Grass
   B) Mushrooms
   C) Pine trees
   D) Dandelions

The correct answer is B:) Mushrooms. Grass, pine trees and dandelions are all producers.

84) What is another term for the gases released due to the burning of fossil fuels?

   A) Smoke
   B) Greenhouse gases
   C) Chemical debris
   D) Toxic fumes

The correct answer is B:) Greenhouse gases.

85) Which steps must a wastewater treatment include in order to be considered a complete treatment?

   I. Preliminary
   II. Primary
   III. Secondary
   IV. Advanced

   A) I and II only
   B) II and III only
   C) I, II and III only
   D) I, II, III and IV

The correct answer is D:) I, II, III and IV. A treatment must contain all four stages (preliminary, primary, secondary, and advanced) to be considered a complete treatment.

86) The practice of rotating what plants are grown on what soil is called

   A) Crop circles
   B) Land management
   C) Food maximizing
   D) Crop rotation

The correct answer is D:) Crop rotation. Crop rotation is the practice of rotating where plants are sown in the earth.

87) Which of the following correctly describes the steps by which a bill becomes a law?

   A) Proposed in one house of Congress, debated, amended, read again, voted on, sent to other house of Congress, debated, amended, read again, voted on, sent to President, signed.
   B) Proposed in one house of Congress, debated, amended, read again, voted, sent to President.
   C) Proposed in one house of Congress, voted on, sent to other house of Congress, voted on, sent to President, signed.
   D) None of the above

The correct answer is A:) Proposed in one house of Congress, debated, amended, read again, voted on, sent to other house of Congress, debated, amended, read again, voted on, sent to President, signed. Answers B and C both leave steps out of the process.

88) When water is nutrient poor it is called

   A) Oligotrophic
   B) Turbid
   C) Murky
   D) Eutrophic

The correct answer is A:) Oligotrophic. When water is nutrient poor it is called oligotrophic.

89) Which term refers to a severe shortage of food?

   A) Famine
   B) Cultural control
   C) Heavy Metals
   D) Aeration

The correct answer is A:) Famine. Famine refers to a severe shortage in food that is accompanied by a significant increase in a population's death rate.

90) What is strip contour cropping?

   A) Planting crops in alternating strips with one being the crop, and another being grass or hay.
   B) Planting crops so that they will grow in neat lines so that space isn't wasted.
   C) Planting crops so that lines go along contours instead of up and down slopes.
   D) Planting crops in alternating strips along contours to minimize soil erosion and effectively use rainfall.

The correct answer is D:) Planting crops in alternating strips along contours to minimize soil erosion and effectively use rainfall. This method is a combination between strip and contour farming.

91) Land that is naturally covered by shallow water at certain times and drained at other times is called

   A) Wetlands
   B) Tidal wetlands
   C) Nontidal wetlands
   D) Flooded lands

The correct answer is A:) Wetlands. Wetlands are land that is naturally covered by shallow water.

92) Which of the following is NOT a waste management method for solid waste?

   A) Nitrification
   B) Incineration
   C) Recycling
   D) Landfills

The correct answer is A:) Nitrification. Nitrification is a step in wastewater treatment, not a waste management method for solid waste.

93) Disease causing bacteria or other viruses are called

   A) Organisms
   B) Pathogens
   C) Insects
   D) Insecticides

The correct answer is B:) Pathogens. Pathogens are disease causing bacteria.

94) The lowest layer of the atmosphere

   A) Tropopause
   B) Stratosphere
   C) Troposphere
   D) Ozone shield

The correct answer is C:) Troposphere. The troposphere is the lowest layer of the atmosphere.

95) The creation or spread of desert

   A) Eutrophication
   B) Turbid
   C) Desertification
   D) Deforestation

The correct answer is C:) Desertification. The spread of desert is called desertification.

96) The accident at Chernobyl effected the future of what?

   A) Cancer research
   B) Nuclear power
   C) Ozone
   D) Military weapons

The correct answer is B:) Nuclear power. The Chernobyl accident made people and politicians anxious about the dangers of nuclear power.

97) When a fish eats another fish and takes on the chemicals inside the fish, compounding them with their own it is called

   A) Desertification
   B) Eutrophication
   C) Deforestation
   D) Biomagnification

The correct answer is D:) Biomagnification. Biomagnification is when a substance becomes concentrated in an organism from its participation in the food chain.

98) In what way do electrostatic precipitators use energy effectively?

   A) They charge all of the air, meaning that it only has to be filtered once to get all the particles.
   B) They charge only the particles, wasting less energy than if all the air was infused.
   C) They charge all of the air, wasting less energy than if all the air was infused.
   D) They charge all of the water in the air, wasting less energy then if the surrounding air was infused.

The correct answer is B:) They charge only the particles, wasting less energy than if all the air was infused.

99) What percent of all manmade CO_2 in the atmosphere is from motor vehicles?

   A) 40%
   B) 50%
   C) 60%
   D) 70%

The correct answer is C:) 60%.

100) Water that is nutrient rich, supporting large amounts of algae is called

   A) Recharge area
   B) Sludge
   C) Eutrophic
   D) Disintegration

The correct answer is C:) Eutrophic.

101) When you are planting crops on a slope to prevent erosion it is called

   A) Farming
   B) Contour cropping
   C) Strip cropping
   D) Land management

The correct answer is C:) Strip cropping. Strip cropping, also called farm cropping is the process of planting crops like hay and wheat in between other crops like soybeans, on a slope to prevent erosion. While A and D could also technically be correct, you are looking for the best and most complete answer.

102) Which of the following is NOT a detrivore?

   A) Earthworms
   B) Termites
   C) Vultures
   D) Birds

The correct answer is D:) Birds. Earthworms, termites and vultures are all considered detrivores.

103) The increase in the world's population has been due to

   A) Increased death rate
   B) Decreased death rate
   C) Increased birth rate
   D) Decreased birth rate

The correct answer is B:) Decreased death rate.

104) A table with a _____ shows when an environment has reached carrying capacity

   A) J curve
   B) S curve
   C) Scattered plot
   D) Bell curve

The correct answer is B:) S curve. An s curve on a chart shows the organisms population until it reaches the carrying capacity of the environment. Once that capacity is reached, it levels off.

105) The sulfur cycle includes which of the following

   A) Combustion of fossil fuels
   B) Volcanic vents
   C) Acid rain
   D) All of the above

The correct answer is D:) All of the above. Sulfur has many forms. These sulfur is produced from the combustion of fossil fuels, volcanic vents and decomposition. When these gasses are released into the atmosphere, it mixes with rain, creating acid rain.

106) Which of the following biogeochemical processes is the slowest?

   A) Water cycle
   B) Nitrogen cycle
   C) Phosphorous cycle
   D) Sulfur cycle

The correct answer is C:) Phosphorous cycle. The phosphorous cycle is the slowest biogeochemical process. This is because phosphorous is released slowly through weathering rocks or decomposition of organisms who had consumed phosphorous.

107) Cultural eutrophication refers to the impact of _____ on eutrophication.

   A) Acid rain
   B) Humans
   C) Fish
   D) All of the above

The correct answer is B:) Humans. Cultural eutrophication is the impact of speeding up eutrophication because of human activity and involvement.

108) Which of the following is a water purification process?

   A) Boiling
   B) Filtering
   C) Bleaching
   D) All of the above

The correct answer is D:) All of the above. Water can be boiled, filtered, or bleached as a way to purify it.

109) What is the Ogallala Aquifer?

   A) A water table located beneath the Great Plains region of the United States.
   B) One of the few remaining Roman aqueducts, which is still used today.
   C) The largest trench in the Atlantic Ocean.
   D) None of the above

The correct answer is A:) A water table located beneath the Great Plains region of the United States.

110) Which of the following is NOT considered mass transit?

   A) Motorcycle
   B) Bus
   C) Lightrail
   D) Subway

The correct answer is A:) Motorcycle. A motorcycle only transports one person, not the masses (lots of people) so it is not considered mass transit.

111) Which of the following is NOT a product crude oil is used in?

   A) Paraffin wax
   B) Plastic
   C) Asphalt
   D) Fertilizer

The correct answer is D:) Fertilizer. Paraffin wax, plastic, and asphalt are all products made in some part with oil.

112) What is strip cropping?

   A) Planting crops in alternating strips with one being the crop, and another being grass or hay.
   B) Planting crops so that they will grow in neat lines so that space isn't wasted.
   C) Planting crops so that lines go along contours instead of up and down slopes.
   D) Planting crops in alternating strips along contours to minimize soil erosion and effectively use rainfall.

The correct answer is A:) Planting crops in alternating strips with one being the crop, and another being grass or hay. By alternating the strips, erosion is minimized.

113) Of the following, which is the most harmful to a water environment?

   A) Decomposition
   B) Oil
   C) Lightrail
   D) Subway

The correct answer is B:) Oil. Crude oil disasters have had a long lasting and detrimental effect on the aquatic environment and the organisms that live in it.

114) Trees protecting crops from wind and soil from erosion are known as

   A) Crop rotation
   B) Agroforestry
   C) Alley cropping
   D) Shelter belts

The correct answer is D:) Shelter belts.

115) The study of the environment and the interaction between it and the organisms that live in it is called

   A) Life science
   B) Biology
   C) Ecology
   D) Economy

The correct answer is C:) Ecology. Ecology is the study of the relationship between organisms and the environment that they live in. While answers A and B are partly correct, ecology is the MOST correct answer.

116) Which of the following is NOT considered mass transit?

   A) Trams
   B) Busses
   C) Carpooling
   D) Subway

The correct answer is C:) Carpooling. Carpooling is not considered mass transit because it is not available to the public in general, but is considered a private agreement.

117) What is ozone?

   A) A form of oxygen which resides in the stratosphere.
   B) A form of oxygen which absorbs radiation from the sun.
   C) A form of oxygen whose chemical formula is O3.
   D) All of the above

The correct answer is D:) All of the above. Answer A, B, and C all correctly describe ozone.

118) Which area of the U.S. has the most incidence of acid rain?

   A) Southwest
   B) Northwest
   C) Southeast
   D) Northeast

The correct answer is D:) Northeast. The northeast has the most incidence of acid rain. This pattern of high acidity is caused by the large number of cities, the dense population, and the concentration of power and industrial plants in the Northeast.

119) Which of the following is absorbed by plants during photosynthesis?

   A) Carbon dioxide
   B) Carbon monoxide
   C) Nitrogen
   D) Oxygen

The correct answer is A:) Carbon dioxide. Carbon dioxide is absorbed by plants during photosynthesis.

120) Which of the following is a colorless, odorless gas that occurs when fossil fuels are not completely burned?

   A) Carbon dioxide
   B) Carbon monoxide
   C) Nitrogen
   D) Oxygen

The correct answer is B:) Carbon monoxide. Carbon monoxide is a colorless, odorless gas that occurs when fossil fuels are not completely burned.

121) Which of the following is NOT true?

   A) The One Birth Policy is an effective way to slow population increase.
   B) Because of the One Birth Policy female children have become subjects of disdain and infanticide.
   C) The One Birth Policy will extend at least through the year 2019.
   D) All of the above are correct statements

The correct answer is D:) All of the above are correct statements. Answers A, B and C are all true statements relating to the One Birth Policy.

122) Which of the following is similar to an underwater ecosystem?

   A) Forest
   B) Lake
   C) Pond
   D) None of the above

The correct answer is D:) None of the above. Deep sea ecosystems are unlike any others because they thrive without sunlight.

123) A series of producers and consumers is also known as a/an

   A) Supply chain
   B) Supply rates
   C) Food chain
   D) All of the above

The correct answer is D:) All of the above. Answer A, B, and C all correctly describe ozone.

124) The process of removing salt from water is known as

   A) Aquifer
   B) Remediation
   C) Desalination
   D) None of the above

The correct answer is C:) Desalination.

125) Areas where freshwater from a river mixes with seawater are known as

   A) Aquifer
   B) Groundwater
   C) Capillary water
   D) Estuaries

The correct answer is D:) Estuaries.

126) Sediment from improperly managed construction sites is an example of

   A) Nonpoint source pollution
   B) Eutrophication
   C) Runoff
   D) Disintegration

The correct answer is A:) Nonpoint source pollution. NPS pollution is caused by rainfall or snow melt moving over and through the ground, picking up pollutants and depositing them in our water sources.

127) Deep water has little or no dissolved oxygen in _____ areas.

   A) Easement
   B) Eutrophic
   C) Estuary
   D) Entropy

The correct answer is B:) Eutrophic.

128) What type of substance is generally referred to when talking about biomagnification?

   A) Biodegradable products
   B) Fossil fuels
   C) Heavy Metals
   D) Insects

The correct answer is C:) Heavy Metals. Heavy metals are generally referred to when discussing the process of biomagnification and bioaccumulation. They build up in the body and be passed from one organism to another.

129) Which of the following is a reason that rain forest soil isn't suitable for planting crops?

   A) There is not enough land area in the world's rain forests to make a suitable farm.
   B) They become exhausted of nutrients relatively quickly.
   C) Areas where rainforests thrive tend to have insufficient rain.
   D) None of the above

The correct answer is B:) They become exhausted of nutrients relatively quickly.

130) In farming, rows of shade-trees are alternated with rows of food or other crops is referred to as

   A) Crop rotation
   B) Agroforestry
   C) Alley cropping
   D) Contour farming

The correct answer is C:) Alley cropping.

131) The heavy material that sinks to the bottom during wastewater treatment is known as what?

   A) Sludge
   B) Scum
   C) Trash
   D) Debris

The correct answer is A:) Sludge. During the primary water treatment process, the material that sinks to the bottom of the tanks is sludge and the lighter material that floats on top of the water is skimmed off and known as scum.

132) _____ is the interaction between two or more factors or substances that yields effects greater than the sum of the individual effects.

   A) Antagonism
   B) Monergism
   C) Synergism
   D) Arminianism

The correct answer is C:) Synergism.

133) Chemosynthesis is the conversion of one or more _____-containing molecules into organic matter using oxidation of inorganic compounds.

   A) Carbon
   B) Nitrogen
   C) Oxygen
   D) Iron

The correct answer is A:) Carbon.

134) _____ is the evolutionary process where organisms that are not closely related manage to develop similar features and traits due to environmental adaptations.

   A) Divergent selection
   B) Convergent selection
   C) Convex selection
   D) Concave selection

The correct answer is B:) Convergent selection. Divergent selection is when common organisms evolve differently and the other answers are fictional.

135) Originally created in 1874 as a means to control malaria and typhus outbreaks, _____ is an insecticide that has become known for its dangerous environmental effects and is banned from use in most countries.

   A) Chlorantraniliprole
   B) Gamma-hexachlorocyclohexane or lindane
   C) Pentachlorophenol
   D) Dichlorodiphenyltrichloroethane or DDT

The correct answer is D:) Dichlorodiphenyltrichloroethane or DDT.

136) The _____ was a series of severe dust storms in the Midwest that damaged American agriculture in the 1930s due to severe drought and failure to apply proper farming methods to prevent erosion.

   A) Rust Bowl
   B) Dust Bowl
   C) Rain Bowl
   D) Prairie Bowl

The correct answer is B:) Dust Bowl. The other answers are variations on the correct answer.

137) The _____ is an international treaty developed in Japan that serves as a framework for reducing greenhouse gas emissions.

   A) Kyoto Protocol
   B) Nagasaki Protocol
   C) Hiroshima Protocol
   D) Osaka Protocol

The correct answer is A:) Kyoto Protocol. Created in 1997, the Kyoto Protocol is an extension of the United Nations Framework Convention on Climate Change (UNFCCC).

138) To dispose of _____ paint, an individual should remove the can lid and let the paint air-dry. The drying process can be sped up by applying an absorbent material.

   A) Water-based
   B) Semi-gloss paint
   C) Oil-based
   D) Satin-based

The correct answer is C:) Oil-based. The other answers are variations on the correct answer or are paint finishes versus types.

139) _____ selection is a type of natural selection where genetic diversity diminishes as the population levels out on a certain trait.

   A) Disruptive
   B) Stabilizing
   C) Directional
   D) Contracting

The correct answer is B:) Stabilizing. Disruptive and directional are other versions of natural selection, while contracting is an incorrect answer.

140) The _____ effect describes the predator/prey interaction, where an increase in predators causes a decrease in prey that leads to a decrease in predators that eventually leads to an increase in prey and so on.

   A) Positive chain
   B) Circular chain
   C) Positive loop
   D) Negative loop

The correct answer is D:) Negative loop. The other answers are variations on the correct answer.

141) The _____ is the theory that shows why two reasonable, rational individuals or businesses may choose not to cooperate with each other even though it is in their best interest to do so.

A) Gamer's dilemma
B) Convict's dilemma
C) Prisoner's dilemma
D) Individual's dilemma

The correct answer is C:) Prisoner's dilemma. The other answers are variations on the correct answer.

 Test-Taking Strategies

Here are some test-taking strategies that are specific to this test and to other DSST tests in general:

- Keep your eyes on the time. Pay attention to how much time you have left.

- Read the entire question and read all the answers. Many questions are not as hard to answer as they may seem. Sometimes, a difficult sounding question really only is asking you how to read an accompanying chart. Chart and graph questions are on most DANTES/DSST tests and should be an easy free point.

- If you don't know the answer immediately, the new computer-based testing lets you mark questions and come back to them later if you have time.

- Read the wording carefully. Some words can give you hints to the right answer. There are no exceptions to an answer when there are words in the question such as always, all or none. If one of the answer choices includes most or some of the right answers, but not all, then that is not the answer. Here is an example:

    The primary colors include all of the following:

    A) Red, Yellow, Blue, Green

    B) Red, Green, Yellow

    C) Red, Orange, Yellow

    D) Red, Yellow, Blue

Although item A includes all the right answers, it also includes an incorrect answer, making it incorrect. If you didn't read it carefully, was in a hurry, or didn't know the material well, you might fall for this.

- Make a guess on a question that you do not know the answer to. There is no penalty for an incorrect answer. Eliminate the answer choices that you know are incorrect. For example, this will let your guess be a 1 in 3 chance instead.

Test Preparation

How much you need to study depends on your knowledge of a subject area. If you are interested in literature, took it in school, or enjoy reading then your study and preparation for the literature or humanities test will not need to be as intensive as that of someone who is new to literature.

This book is much different than the regular DANTES study guides. This book actually teaches you the information that you need to know to pass the test. If you are particularly interested in an area, or feel that you want more information, do a quick search online. We've tried not to include too much depth in areas that are not as essential on the test. Everything in this book will be on the test. It is important to understand all major theories and concepts listed in the table of contents. It is also important to know any bolded words.

Don't worry if you do not understand or know a lot about the area. With minimal study, you can complete and pass the test.

Legal Note

All rights reserved. This Study Guide, Book and Flashcards are protected under the US Copyright Law. No part of this book or study guide or flashcards may be reproduced, distributed or stored in a retrieval system, or transmitted in any form or by any means, electronic, mechanical, photocopying, recording, or otherwise, without the prior written permission of the publisher Breely Crush Publishing LLC.

FLASHCARDS

This section contains flashcards for you to use to further your understanding of the material and test yourself on important concepts, names or dates. Read the term or question then flip the page over to check the answer on the back. Keep in mind that this information may not be covered in the text of the study guide. Take your time to study the flashcards, you will need to know and understand these concepts to pass the test.

Producer	Consumers
Example of a decomposer	Mass transit
Example of a plant that is NOT a consumer	Water is what percentage of the earth?
Troposphere	Energy for all producers and consumers begins with what?

Anything that consumes something else as its source of food	Plants
Busses, trams, subways	Bacteria, worms, bugs
75%	Mushroom
The sun	The first layer of the atmosphere

Omnivores	**Carnivores**
Population	**Carrying Capacity**
Aquatic succession	**The Greenhouse effect says what makes the earth hotter?**
Herbicides	**Insecticides**

Only eat other animals	Eat both plants and animals
The amount of organisms that can be supported in a given area long term	An interbreeding and reproducing group
Trapped gasses	When lakes gradually turn into forests
Chemicals that kill insects	Chemicals that kill plants

DDT was used to control	Erosion
Ogallala Aquifer	Runoff
Which country is the largest producer of trash and consumes the most energy per person?	Watershed
Examples of indoor air pollutants	The Greenhouse effect is also called

When elements like wind and water erode the land	Malaria and body lice
Water that does not seep into the ground through normal channels	A water table located beneath the Great Plains
All the water in a given amount of area	United States
Global Warming	Tobacco smoke, candle smoke, carbon monoxide

Scientists fear that if the temperature continues to rise that	The three R's are
The tracking of hazardous wastes follows the waste from	Ecosystem
Inorganic substances	Organic substances
Humus	All living things are composed of

Re-use, reduce, recycle	The polar ice caps will melt and flood the earth
A group of specific species of plants, animals and microbes that interact with each other	"the cradle-to-the-grave"
Plants, organisms, animals, all living things	Rocks, minerals, gas
Carbon	Dark brown spongy residue from organic materials

Biomagnification	Birth rate is calculated by
Acid rain falls to the earth in	Barren rocks are an example of the location of
Barren farmland is an example of the location of	Turbid
Desertification	Deforestation

Live births divided by 1000 population	When the concentration of a substance increases as it moves through the food chain
Primary succession	Snow, fog, rain
Dark murky water	Secondary succession
When forest is destroyed through cutting and burning	Growth of the desert

40% of landfills is	**Eutrophication**
An electrostatic precipitator	**Eutrophic**
Oligotrophic	**Which country planted 2000 trees?**
Examples of renewable resources	**Stratosphere**

When so many nutrients are brought to a body of water that algae grows abundantly, consuming all the oxygen in the water	Paper
When water is nutrient rich	Electrostatic air cleaner
Australia	When water is nutrient poor
Temperature increases with altitude	Water and solar power

NOTES

NOTES

NOTES

NOTES

NOTES

NOTES

NOTES

NOTES

NOTES

NOTES

NOTES

NOTES

NOTES

NOTES

NOTES

NOTES

NOTES

NOTES

NOTES

NOTES

NOTES

NOTES

NOTES

NOTES

www.ingramcontent.com/pod-product-compliance
Lightning Source LLC
Chambersburg PA
CBHW081832300426
44118CB00014B/2565